COACHING PERSPECTIVES II
Center for Coaching Certification

Cathy Liska

Ruth Dillon

Pamela Lewis

Cynthia Foster

Peggi Peaslee

Erica Torres-Dudziak

Megan Huber

Nicole Stragalas

Sharon Wilcox

Ahfeeyah Thomas

Erick Koshner

Jeanne Hathcock

Dear Reader,

Once again it is a privilege to introduce each Certified Professional Coach who has authored a chapter in this book.

The varied perspectives they offer on the essence of coaching, building a coaching business, and excellence in coaching is an opportunity for expanding awareness and learning more about coaching.

As you read their work, it is clear that they are passionate about sharing their insights. The opportunity to have trained each in coaching and continue to connect with them is an honor.

Kindly let us know how we can be helpful.

Sincerely,

Cathy Liska

Cathy Liska

Guide from the Side™
Center for Coaching Certification

CENTER FOR COACHING CERTIFICATION

www.CenterforCoachingCertification.com

Info@CenterforCoachingCertification.com

800-350-1678

MISSION:
Enhance your coach training experience with
quality, professionalism, and support.

VISION:
A high-quality, ethical norm throughout the coaching
industry achieved through leadership by example.

Table of Contents

For coaches,

those thinking about becoming a coach,

and those who receive coaching.

POWERFUL GOAL SETTING FOR RESULTS
Cathy Liska

Consider how often people set goals and then nothing happens. Choose powerful goal setting for results now.

This chapter explores what is behind powerful goal setting for results by following two individuals. One works with a coach and uses the coaching process, and the other goes with the flow. When part of their story is shared, their name is italicized and in bold. Action steps, indicated with ⇒, are for your use workbook style, so you experience powerful goal setting for results.

To start, make it easy with an acronym:

G = Gigantic
O = Opportunities
A = Analyzed
L = Listed
S = Strategized

Gigantic – is that unrealistic? There are many famous examples of how real gigantic goals are (remember Colonel Sanders started Kentucky Fried Chicken at the age of 65), demonstrating that limitations are often imposed.

Opportunities – how many are there? Reflect for a moment and chances are you remember many conversations where people regret passing on an opportunity.

Analyzed – is it worth spending time on this? It means creating the awareness that supports success.

Listed – on paper? Get specific with what, how, and when.

1

Strategized – how deeply does the thinking go? Intentionally consider what it really takes to make it happen, the timeline, and monitoring.

> ## *"It means creating the awareness that supports success."*

Taking a deeper dive into each these areas supports results. This is done effectively with your business, life, career, or executive coach serving as a sounding board, expanding your thinking, and supporting your planning.

First, it is time to meet *Charlie* and *Ann Marie*.

Charlie is happily married and has two children. He is a really nice guy that everybody likes. Charlie works in corporate America and after years of dedication is bumping up against a move in to management. Charlie's boss recommended he go back to school for a Master's in computer science so that he is prepared for the next level. Charlie talks with his wife. She is very supportive, so he eagerly enrolls. Charlie works hard, studies hard, and struggles to balance family time.

Ann Marie is a newly single mom with one child. She is an office assistant. She is working through the challenges of finalizing her divorce and struggling to make ends meet. Ann Marie's dad has been told he is terminally ill and given a life expectancy of about six months. Because of current life changes, Ann Marie moved recently and knows very few people in the area.

THE G IN GOALS = GIGANTIC

Do people limit themselves? Do you limit yourself? After asking that hundreds of times, it is clear the most common answer is yes. When working with a coach, the coach is completely focused on your success – the coach believes in your abilities. With that kind of unconditional support, you are empowered to move past doubts and the concerns that arise.

> *"...the coach is completely focused on your success – the coach believes in your abilities."*

How do you limit yourself? It starts with thinking – yours and that of others. Humans follow the path of least resistance and that leads downhill, thus creating a tendency to focus on the negative. This in turn limits your expectations. Along the way, life happens and takes you along a path of necessity. Often people around you unintentionally support you in limiting yourself. So can you be successful? A better question is: How do you move past limitations?

It starts with the awareness of what is happening and choosing a different approach. How often have you been asked what you want and invited to really explore and share? Most people tell me they cannot remember that ever happening. A business, life, career, or executive coach asks, and continues to ask and probe, and listens so that you dig deep and consider what really matters to you, what you do want, and what it means to achieve your goals. In and of itself, taking the time to work through what you want is naturally empowering. When someone really listens and then asks follow-up questions in a space that is safe, the experience is amazing.

Charlie tells his wife he wants to move in to management to advance his career and because then he will earn more money.

Ann Marie won three months of coaching in a fundraising raffle. When her coach asked what she wanted, Ann Marie said, "I just want to make enough to take care of my child and live comfortably." Her coach asked her how much she thought was enough for living comfortably. Ann Marie began quantifying – she added up expenses, allowed for emergencies and extras, and then set a goal for her earnings in the next year. The coach then asked about what she wanted to earn further out. For the first time, Ann Marie began to consider moving past survival mode and in to taking charge of creating the life she wanted. Ann Marie and her coach explored goals in all areas of her life.

Specifically, left alone people's goals often remain undefined and the process for achieving the goals undetermined. Dig deeper: If you want enough, how much is enough? What is living comfortably? What else do you want? What does it mean to achieve this? Describe the ideal outcome. Left alone with these questions, it is challenging to really explore fully the answers. Working with a coach who is there for you and focused completely on you means digging deep and expanding your thinking.

⇒ Play with the concept a bit now: With openness for unlimited possibilities, what is your dream? On paper, write down the really basic dreams and ideas first. Next, list your regular, solid, good dreams and plans. Then list great dreams and ideas. Sort what you want into goals for your career, finances, personal life, relationships, health, and lifestyle. Reflect back on your list and in each category, prioritize what you think is most important. Now identify what you want the most.

4

One way for choosing priorities is to reflect: When you retire, what do you want to have done? Think about retired people you know and their successes – what do they value? Now fast forward for yourself: Using the list you created, prioritize what is important and what you want. Now imagine, years from now as you reflect on your life, what is the impact of your priorities? How did each one make a difference? How did your priorities affect other goals in your life? Consider your life a legacy – what legacy do you want to create and leave?

Consider how the choices you make now define your direction and outcomes. Be intentional with your choices and priorities. Dream big and realize that gigantic goals are achievable. When you are aware of what you really want and have fully explored your goals, choose what you will focus on now.

> *"Consider how the choices you make now define your direction and outcomes."*

THE O IN GOALS = OPPORTUNITIES

What are your opportunities for progress towards and then ultimately achievement of your goals? An easy place to start is identifying realistic opportunities you have right now. From there, move to opportunities that are a stretch. Then explore idealistic opportunities.

Charlie has a conversation with his wife over dinner. He states that his next review is coming up in six months and hopefully he will be recommended for a raise or even a promotion. At the very least he will get a cost of living increase. Charlie and his wife will wait hopefully.

Ann Marie wonders if she has an opportunity. Her coach asks for more information. Ann Marie shares that she is unsure of career opportunities where she works and the budget is tight. Her coach asks Ann Marie what other possibilities she wants to explore. Ann Marie says, "Well, I guess I would have to look for a different job somewhere else." With probing, Ann Marie adds to the list of opportunities: Have a conversation with her current employer about possibilities, get a second job, get more training to enhance her résumé, and network to explore other options. Together Ann Marie and her coach explore the options and opportunities. They discuss the pros and cons of each and what it would take to make it happen.

⇒ How does this work for you? Imagine for a moment your goal, like Ann Marie, is a comfortable income. In the previous section this was further explored so the amount of income is defined. To reach that income level, consider your opportunities. A realistic opportunity might be a raise in the current job. The stretch may be a promotion. The ideal may be a higher level position with a different company. Of course for each person what is realistic, a stretch, and an ideal is different – unique to circumstances. For each of your goals, explore your opportunities.

> ## *"For each of your goals, explore your opportunities."*

Further supporting the opportunities requires identifying the resources for achieving goals. This process supports the outcome because when you identify the means for achieving, then the opportunity is more realistic. A business, life, career, or executive coach takes time creating this list with a client because they are aware of the importance. By listing the resources you have and want, your goals become more realistic to you because you are aware of your opportunities, the 'how' behind the dreams.

Ann Marie tells her coach that her resources include her skill set, a few key relationships, time, and a willingness to work hard. Resources she would like include negotiation skills, additional training, and a good résumé.

⇒ With the list of gigantic goals on hand, reflect on the various resources you will use to make it happen. Start by listing the skills you have to achieve your goals (do a bit of digging to get everything listed). Examples include areas of knowledge, work skills, and personal skills. Then list the tools you have to achieve goals. The list might include things like access to training, books, memberships, a computer with internet access, and financial means. Next, list the people that support you and are willing to help you with your goals. The list may include family, friends, colleagues, and supervisors. After listing the resources you have, list resources you want and will use to achieve goals. You'll find that the resources you want are obtainable.

Buy-in is a natural result of going through this process because **G**igantic goals are explored and **O**pportunities defined. A business, life, career, or executive coach realizes that buy-in is essential for long-term results. In powerful goal setting for results, this is as simple as an individual buying into their own goals. Of course this does require moving past limitations and really exploring to decide what you want and the opportunities for achieving it. Further solidifying your success are the next steps of possibilities **A**nalyzed, actions **L**isted, and the process **S**trategized. Now take this a step further – dive deeper.

Ann Marie is asked by her coach to describe her own future success. She imagines feeling confident, secure, relaxed, and happy. The coach continues asking questions for a fuller description. Ann Marie visualizes her child smiling happily and she sees herself living in a small home she owns. Ann Marie says she will hear happy chatter. She imagines telling herself that she did well and accomplished her goals.

⇒ Take a moment now and work through this process. Using the list of goals you wrote, respond to the following:
- Describe your life after achieving what you want.
- What will you see?
- Imagine the expression on your face – describe it.
- What do you see around you?
- What do you hear?
- What are you saying to yourself?
- How does it feel?
- What does it mean to you?

As you explore your own responses, continue to ask, "What else?" with each of the above to ensure it is described fully.

As the ideal outcome is described fully in terms of what is seen, heard, and felt it becomes increasingly real. Coaches realize this creates buy-in, and when you experience it you will find that to be true. This solidifies the possibilities in your opportunities.

> *"As the ideal outcome is described fully in terms of what is seen, heard, and felt it becomes increasingly real."*

THE A IN GOALS = ANALYZED

Thus far you have explored and created **G**igantic goals, then defined the **O**pportunities. Next is **A**nalyzing the 'how' of achieving results. A business, life, career, or executive coach is aware that each person is unique in how they approach planning. Coach training programs include developing skills to identify individual preferences. Additionally, a coach will challenge your thinking and your approach. Consider your steps for research, making decisions, and planning.

Charlie prefers a big-picture understanding. Knowing that the steps for him include his Master's degree, the review process provides him with as much information as he wants.

Ann Marie wants detail. On her own, she will research average pay for her job, how much time and work go in to finding a different job, what education or training is required to advance, how to write a résumé, and what other types of jobs make sense. Ann Marie's coach asks her about her timeline for increasing her income and advancing her career. Ann Marie realizes that if she gets too involved with research it will prevent her moving forward. Next, Ann Marie's coach asks her how she will make her decisions and how detailed her approach will be so she moves forward within her timeline.

⇒ Whatever you prefer, consider the benefits of the various options so that as you move forward your awareness is enhanced.

"...consider the benefits of the various options..."

Specifically, if you prefer the big picture, explore whether some detail is beneficial in making your decisions. If you prefer some detail, decide how much and also analyze from the big picture perspective. If you prefer lots of research, how much time will you allow before making a decision? There is benefit to having a specific procedure, and there is benefit to going with the flow; what is the balance that makes sense for you?

Questions to explore include:

- What level of information works for you?
  - o Do you prefer just the big picture, some detail, or lots of research?
- What decision-making tools will you use?
  - o For example, do you prefer a pro / con list, considering possible outcomes, seeking input then reflecting, analyzing the options, or going with your gut instincts?
- What is your approach?
  - o Is it knowing exactly what you are doing when or going with the flow?

If you have a coach, an additional option is to think out loud and talk it through with the coach listening, reflecting, and asking more questions to enhance your process.

Reflecting on and responding to these questions lays the foundation for how you analyze goals and plan for success. Powerful goal setting for results also means recognizing that challenges exist and will arise. In business, life, career, or executive coaching, the challenges are listed before deciding on the action steps.

Ann Marie is asked by her coach to list potential obstacles to success. Ann Marie thinks that time, the money for additional education or training, the job market, and her lack of connections are her barriers.

⇒ Ask yourself: What are the potential barriers? Through coaching hundreds of individuals over the years, I find some responses come up frequently and are true for many people. What is interesting is that often the very first answer to this question is: Me. This does make sense – we all have tendencies that hold us back, such as procrastination, taking on too much, lacking confidence, being easily distracted, or creating resistance. Beyond that, common barriers include time, money, and knowledge. Continue asking this question: What are the potential barriers? Then ask: What else? Dig, dig, and dig on this question. By getting all of the potential barriers listed, you are empowered to face each one and plan how to move past it.

> *"By getting all of the potential barriers listed, you are empowered to face each one and plan how to move past it."*

After implementing a plan of action, unforeseen barriers may arise, so it is important to come back to the process of listing the barriers and then, with each barrier foreseen or unforeseen, ask the next question: How will you move past it?

When working with a coach, initially moving past each barrier is explored, and then moving past barriers is shifted to the whole approach of the action planning. Consider the benefit of this approach with a coach or for yourself – in the short term it means being prepared and in the long term it means focusing on planning and following through.

11

Next, **A**nalyze three very significant considerations when focusing on powerful goal setting for results – how the goal is defined, motivation, and action.

How the goal is defined: Many people find it easier to describe what they do not want than to describe what they do want. For example, someone might say, "I don't want to be so stressed any more." Or perhaps, "I am tired of always struggling to pay the bills." When describing what is not wanted, the brain processes the key words – in these examples 'stressed' and 'struggling to pay bills'. The focus is on the very thing that is not wanted and it continues to be true. When the goal is described as what is wanted, there is a shift. For example, saying, "I want to relax," or "I want to afford things easily," the brain focuses on the key words 'relax' and 'afford easily'. By focusing forward, on what is wanted, the brain is given an actual goal and achieving results is easier.

> ## *"When the goal is described as what is wanted, there is a shift."*

Motivation: If a goal is based on external factors, such as consequences, or what others think or want, buy-in and follow-through are short-term and success is limited. A business, life, career, or executive coach will ask a client what achieving a particular goal means to them personally. Recognizing the value personally creates buy-in and increases follow-through.

Action: When waiting for something to happen or for others to take an action in order to achieve a goal, chances are the waiting goes on and on. When owning outcomes and intentionally considering what action is controllable, progress begins and continues. Powerful goal setting for results means proactively planning and acting.

> ## *"Powerful goal setting for results means proactively planning and acting."*

Charlie wants to not worry about paying his bills each month. He feels that his family depends on him to earn a good living. He is following the advice of his boss and waiting for the next step in the process.

Ann Marie is challenged by her coach to define what she does want and says financial security plus a career that is challenging and rewarding. Ann Marie is asked to state how these goals are important to her, and she tells her coach that she will feel safe and be proud of herself. Ann Marie works with her coach to plan what action steps she will take to support her long term success.

⇒ Review your list of goals and be sure each is defined in terms of what you do want, your internal motivation is known, and that you are proactively planning action steps.

THE L IN GOALS = LISTED

Now that you have **G**igantic goals with **O**pportunities to achieve them and **A**nalyzed how you will create your process, it is time to begin **L**isting specifics. Whether with a business, life, career, or executive coach or here now, begin by developing a timeline.

Charlie believes that his entire career will be with the same company and that raises and promotions are based on what is happening with the company. He likes to plan his budget each year and then track it monthly.

Ann Marie realizes that she has short-term requirements for taking care of her child and herself. She also wants to start working on her future now. With her coach, Ann Marie determines that covering her immediate expenses is a top priority and she wants to begin working on the goal of a higher income so that she will achieve it within two years. To support her long-term goal of a rewarding career, Ann Marie plans to begin researching options.

⇒ How far in advance do you want to plan? Using your list of goals, sort each of the goals in to one of three categories:

- Short-term: within a year
- Mid-term: the next 2-4 years
- Long-term: 5 years or longer

While it makes sense to jump on planning for the short-term goals, consider also what steps now set you up for success with your mid-term and long-term goals.

> *"...steps now set you up for success with your mid-term and long-term goals."*

Reflect on your reasons for listing goals in each of these categories. How did you choose the short-term goals? Possibilities include necessity, ease, urgency, or desire. What is

14

the reason goals are categorized as mid-term? It may be so that you have time to gather resources or because of circumstances. How did you decide which goals are long-term? Considerations include the size of the goal, the amount of work required, or simply the process to achieve it taking time. Tap the knowledge of excellent coaches: understanding reasons for the timelines, combined with recognizing which goals require action and when, prepares you to list your steps for success.

Life is busy for most people and powerful goal setting for results takes time and effort – it makes sense that it is easy to get off track. Business, life, career, and executive coaches realize that the listing of goals and 'to do' items supports focus and staying on track for success.

The level of list building varies based on personal style – what works is different for each person.

Powerful goal setting for results includes using one or more of the following levels:

- Monthly 'to do's'
  This list includes all of the 'to do' items you want to accomplish within the next month, and is left open-ended with the idea that as long as it is on the list you will take care of it.

- Weekly 'to do's'
  The next level of a list is to pull from the monthly 'to do' items and create a list of what you will accomplish each week.

- Daily 'to do's'
  Once a week, using your weekly schedule, list 'to do' items based on which day you will accomplish each.

Additionally, sometimes it is effective to list the exact time an action step will be taken.

Charlie feels that daily or even weekly 'to do' lists are tedious. He prefers a monthly and an annual list. He and his wife create their lists and talk about them periodically.

Ann Marie realizes that her tendency is to have monthly checklists and she sometimes pushes things back each month. Her coach encourages her to experiment with daily and weekly checklists. Ann Marie finds that she is excited about marking things on her list as complete and it motivates her to keep going.

⇒ Using your list of gigantic goals with opportunities for achieving them that you analyzed, create a comprehensive checklist of 'to do' items.

Now dive in to discover what is behind powerful action steps in a procedural, detailed approach. When a 'to do' item or action step is detailed, it is easily understood and completed. For example, rather than simply planning to communicate with a colleague, dig deeper: How will you communicate with them? When will you communicate with them? Hence, instead of listing 'communicate with colleague', the action step becomes to call them on Tuesday at 10 AM.

> *"When a 'to do' item or action step is detailed, it is easily understood and completed."*

Recognize whether each action step is doable. For example, if you are scheduled to be in a meeting on Tuesday at 10 AM, then the above action step is unlikely. Of course, doable goes beyond basic scheduling – it also means that you have the resources and knowledge, and where others are involved that they are available, willing, and able too.

For many people, a general timeline or 'to do' list works, and for others, defining the specific date and time is more effective. Whichever works best for you, whether with a coach or individually, schedule time to create your checklist and/or calendar specific, doable action steps.

THE S IN GOALS = STRATEGIZED

Thus far, you have explored **G**igantic goals, **O**pportunities for success, **A**nalyzed your process, and **L**isted your action steps. This is part of developing your **S**trategy of powerful goal setting for results. Business, life, career, and executive coaches realize that while many people want things to happen now, it takes understanding what works, how it works, and following through.

> *"...it takes understanding what works, how it works, and following through."*

By following this process, you have taken a step to begin your new journey: you explored your dreams and believe in your goals; you considered your possibilities, developed your process, and wrote a 'to do' list of action steps. If you are planning to do

17

this later, when will you start? After you start, what happens? When you have a coach, one thing they do is check in with you on how you are doing to ensure accountability.

Specifically, in your strategizing or with your coach, plan regular intervals to reflect on what is and is not working. Define this so that you continue doing what works and adjust for what doesn't work. For example, if your action plan included steps to earn a promotion and then you did not get the promotion, explore the reasons. Under "what did not work" might be specific tasks you took on to demonstrate your value and they turned out to be low-profile. Under "what did work" might be skill development that resulted in productivity improvements. By exploring both, you have the knowledge to adjust your plan effectively and continue moving toward your goals.

> *"...plan regular intervals to reflect on what is and is not working."*

Charlie feels good about his job, his family, and his life. He believes he is moving forward and with time will continue to advance.

Ann Marie begins working on her plan and runs in to a few glitches. She feels overwhelmed and slows down. Then her coach asks how she is doing, what is working, and what is holding her back. Ann Marie explains the problems preventing her progress. Her coach asks her how she will move past the challenges. Ann Marie regains her focus and realizes that she will continue to make progress.

18

⇒ Using your list of action steps, answer these questions for yourself. What checkpoints make sense? What are your preferences for managing accountability? How will you stay on track and continue your progress when faced with challenges?

Powerful goal setting for results includes the tips included here for exploring **G**igantic goals, **O**pportunities for success, **A**nalyzing your process, **L**isting action steps, and **S**trategizing effort. A plan is good – using the plan is awesome and gets results. Now, imagine for a moment that someone you know and trust gave you the ideal plan for your life and achieving success. Would you be committed to making it happen? Chances are…no. When you create the plan, chances are yes. Ultimately, as business, life, career, and executive coaches realize, commitment comes from within and commitment is key for achieving results.

> ## *"A plan is good – using the plan is awesome and gets results."*

Charlie feels he is committed to advancing in his career and earning more money. His wife is supportive and believes in him. Charlie is doing what his boss asked.

Ann Marie realizes that between finalizing her divorce, supporting her mom in caring for her dad, dealing with her own grief, and ensuring stability for her child, it would be easy to put her goals on the back burner. Through coaching she develops awareness that her commitment to her goals now is the difference between getting by throughout her life and creating a good life for her child and herself.

⇒ Ask yourself: What is your commitment to making it happen? How do you feel about your goals? How do you feel about your plan? What does it do for you? What is the benefit and value?

Perhaps you have heard the saying about how attitude is the determining factor for altitude: If you are hesitant, unsure, or doubtful, your chances for success are minimized. If you are excited and enthusiastic, and convinced your plan is great, you will make it happen.

⇒ Dig deeper: What is your level of energy for working on your goals? Sometimes energy is negative or controlled by external factors – this results in short-term and limited progress. When your energy is positive and controlled internally, success is achieved more efficiently and easily. It is possible to choose positive, internally controlled energy – just ask a coach!

Will you make the effort to achieve what you want? Using the process described here, ideally with the support of a great coach, commitment, and positive energy, it is easier to achieve more – and the paradox is that because of the impact of this process you are willing to put in more effort!

Part of strategizing is deciding how you will measure success. When you do achieve the measurement, are you aware of it? Take the time to recognize what you have accomplished! Valuing and respecting yourself through recognizing and rewarding both progress and success supports your long-term motivation and bigger successes.

> *"Take the time to recognize what you have accomplished!"*

Charlie really appreciates the support of his wife and feels good about his work and life. When he does get a big raise or promotion, he knows they will celebrate together.

Ann Marie realizes that she is so wrapped up in daily living that she forgets to think about how much she has accomplished. The idea of celebrating success seems so far in the future. When her coach asks how she is doing with her action steps, Ann Marie shares what she has completed. She is surprised to discover how meaningful it is when her coach congratulates her for her progress. When her coach asks about celebrating her success, Ann Marie thinks and decides that she would like to take a trip with her child. When Ann Marie defines how she will reward herself, her commitment and motivation are enhanced.

⇒ How will you know you have achieved the results? Define how you measure success. Be specific and list what has to happen for you to realize you accomplished your goal. How will you reward yourself? Create a plan for acknowledging your progress and celebrating your success!

Now please allow me to ask: Are you using and applying this information?

If yes – excellent! Please pay forward the benefit by sharing on the Center for Coaching Certification Facebook page *(http://www.facebook.com/CoachingCertification?ref=ts)* or LinkedIn group *(http://www.linkedin.com/groups/Center-Coaching-Certification-3013346?home=&gid=3013346&trk=anet_ug_hm)*.

If no – what is holding you back? Would you benefit from having a coach? Visit www.FindaCertifiedCoach.com or www.CenterforCoachingSolutions.com for access to hundreds of Certified Professional Coaches.

What have you learned from this chapter? How has it benefitted you? Share your stories online or send us an email – whether you are a coach reviewing the concepts from the coach training program or an individual applying these ideas in your life.

Key concepts from coach training on powerful goal setting for results provide an amazing process to achieve success:

- Explore what you really want by moving past imposed limitations and thinking with an open spirit – dream big and list **G**igantic goals you want to reflect back on having achieved years from now.
- Discover your **O**pportunities, list your resources, and describe your ideal outcome.
- **A**nalyze your process, barriers, and focus.
- **L**ist your goals on a timeline, develop a checklist, and define your action steps.
- **S**trategize your journey from beginning to end with commitment, and celebrate success

The chapter is the full guide – and the quick reference is:

G = Gigantic dreams
O = Opportunities for success
A = Analyzed process
L = Listed steps
S = Strategized effort

Best Wishes on Your Powerful Goal Setting for Results!

Cathy Liska is the founder of the Center for Coaching Certification, Find a Certified Coach, and the Center for Coaching Solutions.

Her coaching niche areas include Business Development, Communication and Conflict, and Intentional Living.

As the Guide from the Side™, she is recognized among the best internationally in training, coaching, conflict mediation, and consulting. Cathy has presented, trained, and facilitated thousands of events, workshops, certification courses, and organizational retreats. She freely shares from her 20 years of experience in business ownership and management.

To ensure she continues to stay current in related fields and areas of expertise, Cathy has earned the following designations: Certified Master Coach Trainer, Certified Professional Coach, Certified Consumer Credit Counselor, Real Estate Broker, Certified Apartment Manager, Certified Family Mediator, Certified Civil Mediator, Certificate of Excellence in Nonprofit Leadership and Management, Certified in the Drucker Self-Assessment Tool, Grief Support Group Facilitator, and Certified Trainer/Facilitator.

Cathy's personal mission statement is "People". Cathy is known for her passion in sharing the insight, experience, positive attitude, and information that empower others to achieve the results they desire.

www.CenterforCoachingCertification.com
Cathy@CenterforCoachingCertification.com
800-350-1678

TWO EXPERTS IN THE COACHING PROCESS

Ruth Dillon

There are two experts in the coaching process: the coach and the client. The coach may mistakenly be perceived as the expert, similar to a consultant. A consultant is a content expert; a coach is a process expert. In a consulting relationship, the client pays for expertise in content. Conversely, in a coaching relationship the client *is* the expert in content so is paying for the coach's expertise in process. This creates a purposeful conversation to facilitate accomplishment of the client's desired results.

During coaching, the client is working honestly to introspectively explore, clarify, and overcome their own objections to meeting their goals. The coach is asking powerful questions – clarifying, probing, and open questions – that are supportive in meeting client goals.

The coach, regardless of what type of coach, draws out the client through respectful and useful questions. Importantly, the coach – particularly the transformational coach – notices opportunities to ask a question that could potentially create a positive shift in client attitude, belief, or behavior so as to free the client to move closer toward goal attainment and sustainability of results.

> *"There are two experts in the coaching process:*
> *the coach and the client."*

CLIENT AS EXPERT IN CONTENT

The client is the expert on the content of their life experiences. The client has a good sense of what it is they want or the reasons they are being urged forward at this time in their life. The client also knows their own values and standards. They know when they resist, and they also realize that they have ineffective attitudes, beliefs, and behaviors – or habits – which block goal attainment. The client generally knows their buttons or triggers. They know their good (values, good intentions, morals), their bad (not living up to their own standards), and their ugly (shame). The bottom line: The client is most familiar with themselves. Sometimes they are aware of what is keeping them from getting what they want and still continue supporting that block. Sometimes they are simply unable to obtain their goals due to lack of focus. Other times they get off track from their goals. It is the client's honesty with themselves in a trusting relationship with a caring and supportive coach, combined with action, that leads the client to their desired results.

The client's expertise in content is integral to the coaching relationship.

COACH AS EXPERT IN PROCESS

The coach is the expert in creating a safe, trusting space for the client to speak honestly and freely with awareness that it is confidential. The coach asks intentional questions of the client while attending to the client and the client's content, often reflecting what the client has just said. In a sense, the client is the teacher and in teaching they expand their own awareness. The coach learns about the client in order to most effectively support them. In this relationship, the coach holds a philosophical stance that the client has their own answers and is resourceful and creative.

As an expert in process, the coach is a facilitator who supports the client to discover their answers and to creatively link with their resources. The coach walks with the client, side by side, based on the *client's* agenda. The coach asks questions – the coach's main tool – to draw out the client (to induce the client to speak freely), to have the client clarify (to free themselves from ambiguity), to have the client probe (to examine closely), and to ultimately create the possibility of a positive client-owned shift in attitudes, beliefs, and behavior.

The coach ensures that the client is in the driver's seat to thoughtfully respond to the questions on their own terms. In fact, the client is free to request a different question. In this collaborative process, the coach supports the client to get clear about what they want, what their resources and timelines are, and how they will go about achieving their desired results. If the client is only partially buying in to their goals or they get stuck or off track from progress, the coach uses shift-creating questions for the possibility of new realizations which then free up the client to move closer to their desired results.

The coach's expertise in process is integral to the coaching relationship.

Now let's observe a sampling of a session between a young businesswoman and a transformational life coach.

> *"The coach ensures that the client is in the driver's seat to thoughtfully respond to the questions on their own terms."*

SAMPLE COACHING SESSION

Coach: Earlier in the session you established that you want a healthy lifestyle. What exactly do you mean by that? *<clarifying question>*

Client: I want to start an exercise program. *<content>*

Coach: Good! What are some of your ideas for doing that? *<drawing out question>*

Client: I'm thinking about joining a new gym near work because they're advertising for a free personal trainer for three months with a one-year membership. *<content>*

Coach: Great! I noticed you said you're *thinking* about joining the gym? *<clarifying question, opportunity to create a shift>*

Client: Right. I don't really trust myself to stick with it to get my money's worth. That's partly why I wanted to hire a coach because then I won't be able to hide. *<content>*

Coach: So, in addition to wanting a coach, you want to start an exercise program, you're thinking of joining the nearby gym that offers the free personal trainer with membership, and you want to trust yourself to stick with it, right? *<clarifying question>*

Client: Exactly! The worst part is not trusting myself. *<content>*

Coach: May I ask you about that? *<permission question>*

Client: Sure! *<content>*

Coach: What prevents you from trusting yourself? *<probing question, opportunity to create a shift>*

Client: I'm not trusting myself to go to the gym to work out. *<content>*

Coach: Okay. May I ask you some more questions to support you in trusting yourself with this? *<permission question>*

Client: Yes, please do. *<content>*

Coach: Thank you. What are the reasons you don't trust yourself to go to the gym to work out? *<probing question>*

Client: Well, I've joined gyms before with lifetime memberships and then only went a few times. *<content>*

Coach: Okay. So what is it that had you go to the gym only a few times? *<probing question>*

Client: The fact that I didn't know what I was doing on the machines and also not having any real goals. *<content>*

Coach: Okay, and you also said you could get a personal trainer with a new gym membership; what's your interest in that? *<drawing out question>*

Client: Oh, I think I'll be much more likely to go if there's a personal trainer there. *<content>*

Coach: What is it about a personal trainer that is motivating for you? *<drawing out question>*

Client: Because I imagine I'll have appointed times to be there, and I don't miss appointments. *<content>*

Coach: Okay. What else? *<drawing out question>*

Client: Because I think that the personal trainer will help me learn how to use the machines. *<content>*

Coach: Yes. What other reasons are you more likely to go if there's a personal trainer? *<drawing out question>*

Client: Because I'll probably have to set goals and will probably make better progress since they will track my results. *<content>*

Coach: Okay, what else? *<drawing out question>*

Client: That's all.

Coach: Now what about after that first three months when there is no more free personal trainer? *<drawing out question>*

Client: I'm happy to pay for it if I still need one after three months. *<content>*

Coach: And what would cause you to want a personal trainer after three months? *<probing question>*

Client: I think I'll want one if my goals aren't met or if I still need the appointment to get me there. *<content>*

Coach: Okay. So you'd be willing to hire a personal trainer after three months if you felt this keeps you on track? *<clarifying question to cement client buy-in>*

Client: Yes, that's correct. *<content>*

Coach: And if your goals are met, what then? *<drawing out question>*

Client: I'll have the personal trainer help me maintain the weight I lose. *<content>*

Coach: Oh, so in addition to wanting to start an exercise program, it sounds like you also have a weight goal? *<clarifying question>*

Client: Yes. I want to lose 20 pounds. *<content>*

Coach: Okay, so that would put you at what weight? *<clarifying and permission question>*

Client: Around 130 pounds. *<content>*

Coach: Okay, by when do you want this new weight? *<probing question>*

Client: Actually, a three-month timeframe is perfect for me at about two pounds off per week. *<content>*

Coach: Okay. Now let me back up for a minute, okay? *<permission question>*

Client: Sure! *<content>*

Coach: So what's the value to you of working with a transformational life coach at the same time you're working with a personal trainer? *<clarifying question>*

Client: Well, a personal trainer can support me in reaching my exercise and weight loss goals. I feel like I still want a coach to support me when I get off track. *<content>*

Coach: Okay. I noticed you said "when" you get off track; what would cause you to get off track? *<probing question and opportunity to create a shift>*

Client: I'm afraid I could do all this with the gym membership and personal trainer and then just gain it all back. *<content>*

Coach: What do you think would prevent you from staying on track? *<probing question>*

Client: By overeating. *<content>*

Coach: Now what would cause that? *<probing question>*

Client: I get anxious at work when I have to make a tough decision and then I turn to comfort foods like pastries and cookies. *<content>*

Coach: So it sounds like you'd like to do some work on shifting this behavior so that you turn to something healthy? *<permission question and opportunity to create a shift>*

Client: Yes, exactly. I want to finally break the habit of turning to comfort foods when I'm faced with a tough decision. *<content>*

Coach: Okay, would you like to actually work on this right now? *<permission question>*

Client: Sure, let's go for it! *<content>*

Coach: Okay, what are your ideas for changing the habit? *<drawing out question>*

Client: I have no idea! *<content>*

Coach: Okay. Now if you *were* to know, what would your ideas be? Take your time, and give it your best. *<drawing out question, opportunity to create a shift>*

Client: Hmm. Let me think. Oh, I know! I would first need to believe I can do it! *<content, client realization>*

Coach: Good. What will it take in order to believe you will be successful at changing this habit? *<drawing out question, opportunity to create a shift>*

Client: Oh my goodness! I need to give myself some success with it! *<content, client realization>*

Coach: And what are your ideas for doing that? *<drawing out question>*

Client: Well, I guess I'd have to do something other than eat comfort foods next time I feel anxious about a decision. *<content, client realization>*

Coach: So what will you do when you are facing a decision? *<drawing out question>*

Client: What will I do? Well, I can take a break. *<content>*

Coach: Yes! What else? *<drawing out question>*

Client: I can take some deep breaths to soothe myself. *<content>*

Coach: Good! What else will you do? *<drawing out question>*

Client: I will take a moment and get a better perspective on whatever is making me anxious. *<content>*

Coach: Great! What else? *<drawing out question>*

Client: I'll chew a piece of gum. *<content>*

Coach: Okay, good! What else will you do? *<drawing out question>*

Client: I'll eat a piece of fruit. *<content>*

Coach: Good! What else? *<drawing out question>*

Client: I'll stop having the comfort foods around me. *<content>*

Coach: Sure – have different options! What else will you do when you're dealing with a tough decision? *<drawing out question>*

Client: Good grief! I will go to the gym and work out while I think through the decision! *<content, client realization>*

Coach: Yes! Great! What else? *<drawing out question>*

Client: Whew, I think I've got enough ideas now! *<content>*

Coach: Super! Now what are you realizing so far? *<drawing out question to cement client buy-in>*

Client: I'm realizing, thank you, that I have lots of easy options whenever I get that strong urge to eat those comfort foods— meaning that I can choose something else. *<content>*

Coach: Okay good. Now let's go a little deeper with this, okay? *<permission question>*

Client: Sure! *<content>*

Coach: So, with lots of easy options, what will choosing something else do for you? *<drawing out question to cement buy-in>*

Client: Well, if I keep choosing something different, after a while the habit will just be different! *<content, client realization>*

Coach: Yes! And what will changing this habit give you? *<drawing out question to cement client buy-in>*

Client: Well, I'll be gaining self-trust. *<content>*

Coach: Great insight! What will self-trust do for you? *<drawing out question>*

Client: Hmm. What will self-trust do for me? I've never thought about it that way. I guess I'll finally trust myself— period! *<content, client realization>*

Coach: Great! And when you trust yourself, what will that give you? *<drawing out question to cement client buy-in>*

Client: That will give me freedom, and it doesn't get any better than that! *<content, client realization>*

Coach: Great realization! Thank you for being so open. Now, what have you gained from this? *<drawing out question to cement client buy-in>*

Client: So now I realize that when I just choose from one of the easy options, the old habit will eventually end and be replaced by a new healthy one. It all starts with believing I can do this, and I will do that by giving myself a few successes each time I have a challenging decision to make. I'm confident I will do this! *<content>*

Coach: I noticed you are focused on what you are going to do now. *<drawing out question, opportunity to create a shift>*

Client: Yes, I'm already believing I will do this! *<content, client realization>*

Coach: Great! Then you've already taken the first step. What else have you gained from today's session? *<drawing out question to cement client buy-in>*

Client: Oh, well, I believe I can reach my goal of 130 pounds by joining the gym and hiring a personal trainer. I believe I will change my eating to a new healthy habit. I also know this will be challenging for me. *<content>*

Coach: What wonderful gains! Now say more about the challenge you're expecting. *<drawing out statement, opportunity to create a shift>*

Client: I'm in such a habit of feeding my cravings, especially when I feel anxious, that it will take self-control for me to do something different. *<content>*

Coach: Yes. What will it take to meet your challenge for self-control? *<drawing out question, opportunity to create a shift>*

Client: I just want to give this to myself. I want to trust myself. Mainly, I just want to make sure to do something different and to remember the reasons it's important to do something different. *<content, client shift>*

Coach: How will you make sure to do something different? *<drawing out question, opportunity to create a shift>*

Client: You know what? I know I'll do something different, no matter how strong the urge, because it's important to me! *<content, client shift>*

Coach: That's great! Say the reasons doing something different is important to you. *<drawing out statement, opportunity to create a shift>*

Client: It's important to me to change this habit once and for all because of how it affects my self-confidence. It's really important to me to trust myself, and this is a lab for me to do it. Thank you for asking me about that! *<content, client realization>*

Coach: You're so welcome! I'm really glad you're tying your lab work to your value of self-trust. Please say more about your lab work. *<clarifying statement and drawing out question, opportunity to create a shift>*

Client: Okay. Let me think. Okay, my lab work is to change the habit to a healthy one. So to do that I will notice when I'm feeling anxious about making a decision, notice when I get the urge to reach for comfort foods, and then instead, go for one of my easy options. Each time I choose an option, I'll be giving myself more trust that I will keep doing it. And when I give myself more and more trust, my self-confidence will improve too. *<content, client realization>*

Coach: Wow! So tell me: How important is that to you, on a scale of 1 to 10 with 10 being most important? *<probing question to cement client buy-in>*

Client: It's an 11 because it's the world to me! Being successful at this will give me my freedom! *<content>*

Coach: Yes! And when you have self-trust and self-confidence with this, what do you imagine will happen elsewhere in your life? *<drawing out question, opportunity to create a shift>*

Client: I'll likely have the self-trust and self-confidence to handle just about anything! Wow! *<content, client realization>*

Coach: Excellent! Okay, good. So, when we meet again next week I'll ask you about your progress and improvements with changing the habit, okay? *<permission question>*

Client: You bet! *<content>*

Coach: One more thing today: What is your process for tracking your results? *<drawing out question to cement client buy-in>*

Client: I'll journal daily about the times I chose a healthy option. *<content>*

Coach: Great! What will journaling do for you? *<probing question to cement client buy-in>*

Client: It will keep me aware of my lab work. *<content>*

Coach: What will this awareness give you? *<drawing out question to cement client buy-in>*

Client: Focus. *<content>*

Coach: And what will focus give you? *<drawing out question to cement client buy-in>*

Client: Better probability for results. *<content>*

Coach: Okay. Now what will better probability for results give you? *<drawing out question to cement client buy-in>*

Client: What I'm after! *<content>*

Coach: And say one more time—what is it you're after? *<drawing out question to cement client buy-in>*

Client: I'm after self-trust, self-confidence and freedom! And weighing 130 would be nice, too! *<content, client realization>*

Coach: Okay then. Are you complete for now? *<caring, completion question>*

Client: Yes, and thank you so much! *<content>*

Coach: You're so welcome! We'll talk at the same time next week. Have a fruitful week...pun intended! *(laughter)*

Client: Bye now!

Coach: Bye!

DISCUSSION OF THE COACH'S PROCESS

Now let's discuss the coach's process as illustrated in the sample coaching session. Using open-ended and informed questions as the coach's primary tool, the coach listened with care to the client. Through questioning with care and respect, the coach learned much about the client; more importantly, the client explored, clarified, and realized much about *herself* and made shifts in attitudes and beliefs, setting up transformational behavioral shifts. The listening-questioning process generated a shift in client attitude from resignation about ability to break a lifelong sabotaging habit to a new belief by generating simple ways to replace the habit with positive (and easy) behaviors, perhaps for the first time. The process also facilitated the client's shift from disbelieving she could do it to believing that she will; she believes that the gym membership, the personal trainer, the exercise

37

program, the weight maintenance program for hire, and her lab work to cultivate self-trust and self-confidence are all worth her time, effort, and money. Once she made the internal shifts, she focused on moving toward what she wanted and that which supports her success.

"The listening-questioning process generated a shift..."

With a shift in client attitude and belief, what follows is a shift in behavior to reach for positive alternatives. The client said she would like to weigh around 130 pounds by the end of three months; she later said that it's more about self-trust than the weight. This was revealed as a result of her trust, openness, and honesty together with the coach's stance, care, and informed listening-questioning process.

Notice how the coach maintained the philosophical stance that the client has her own answers and is resourceful and creative. When the client exclaimed, "I have no idea!" to the question "What are your ideas for changing the habit?" the coach trusted that she did, in fact, know and gently urged her forward with a new question. "Now if you *were* to know, what would your ideas be?" After some thought, the client responded, "I would first need to believe I can do it!" This was a transformational moment! The coach avoided giving suggestions and effectively stayed out of the way, which allowed the client to experience her own process in a fluid and meaningful way.

In the process, the client effectively tied her desire for self-control to her value of self-trust, which created a motivating buy-in for her to find easy (and healthy) ways of dealing with her feelings in times of tough decision-making. This tying to values was precisely what created positive and meaningful shifts for the client. Suddenly her motivation increased: "I know I'll do something different, no matter how strong the urge, because it's important to me!" The client learned about herself, "It's an 11 because it's the world to me! Being successful at this would give me my freedom!"

> ## "The client learned about herself..."

The coach staying out of the way made room for client buy-in of the real possibility of achieving of her desired results. Client buy-in supports empowered and long-lasting results. The client said she wants to make sure to do something different in response to the question, "What will it take to meet your challenge for self-control?" The coach then asked her to say the reasons it is important to her to do something different. That is when the client realized, "because of how it affects my self-confidence." Further, she asserted, "It's really important for me to trust myself, and this is a lab for me to do it."

The coach encouraged the client to say more about her realizations, further cementing the client's newly empowered beliefs about actualizing the goal. To support client progress, the coach asked her, "What is your process for tracking your results?" to which she responded, "I'll journal daily about the times I chose a healthy option..." The coach saw yet another opportunity to go a step further in cementing client buy-in by asking what journaling would do for her. Ultimately the client responded with awareness, focus, and "What I'm after! Self-trust, self-confidence, and freedom!" Finally, the coach set the expectation

39

for the client to make progress when the coach asked her to be prepared to report on progress and improvements at the next session.

CLIENT AND COACH AS EXPERTS IN THE COACHING PROCESS

The client and the coach are in a symbiotic relationship. The expertise of each is integral to this meaningful, generative, and potentially life-changing process called coaching, which is for the client.

In a nutshell, the client is the one who is ready for a positive change in an area of their life in which they have been less than successful at achieving on their own, and one who is willing to pay for the coach's expertise in process. The client chooses a coach who is a good fit for them in terms of trust, coaching style, scheduling, and price. The client is generally fairly clear about what they want to achieve from coaching, is open to learn more about themselves, and is motivated to succeed in achieving. With the coach's support, the client sets reachable goals for themselves and takes consistent action toward goal attainment. The client shares their successes with the coach, and more importantly their obstacles to success. Because they want to grow, the client is motivated to recognize and shift the attitudes, beliefs, and behaviors which no longer serve them. To do this, they must be respected, heard, and cared about by their coach in such a way that their own buy-in for making the shifts occurs.

"The client and the coach are in a symbiotic relationship."

The coach empowers the client's success by working with the client to explore wants and dreams, to develop reachable goals, to clarify potential challenges or obstacles to goal achievement, to discover ways to move through them, to state session gains for client buy-in, and to take new, effective steps between sessions. The coach supports the client in getting what they want faster and easier than they would likely do on their own, if at all.

There are truly two experts in the coaching process: The client is the expert on content, and the coach is the expert on process. The coach is distinct from an advisor; advice is discovered by the client within the context. The coach is distinct from a consultant; providing expertise in content happens and is separated from the coaching. The coach is distinct from a therapist; coaching can certainly be insightful and therapeutic. The coach draws out the client for the possibility of creating a shift from what hasn't been working to what will now work, which often provides long-lasting freedom from self-limitations. The coach considers themselves a guest in the client's world, and a temporary one at that. The coach is honored to be in such a trusting and rewarding relationship.

The client's expertise in content, combined with the coach's expertise in process, makes for a dynamic and winning team!

As sole proprietor of Ruth Dillon Life Coaching, Ruth facilitates and supports her clients in living a more personally freeing life aligned with what matters most to them. Ruth coaches in a unique shift-creating process called Reflective Questioning, created, developed and mastered over two decades by Marianne Weidlein, CPC, who resides in Denver, Colorado. Reflective Questioning begins with the *client's* question about something in need of the client's understanding and, with the facilitator's support, self-limiting barriers of negative thoughts, beliefs, and perceptions are removed as the client experiences clarity and new realizations. Ruth so believes in the power of Reflective Questioning that she continues her own work with Marianne in support of self-mastery.

Ruth holds a Master of Arts degree in Behavioral Science from the University of Houston-Clear Lake and was in private practice as a Marriage and Family Therapist for many years. Her interest as a coach began when, as a client, she personally experienced the long-lasting effectiveness of coaching, and she earned the Certified Professional Coach designation from the Center for Coaching Certification.

Prior to her career as a therapist and later a coach, Ruth co-founded and co-owned Team Building Systems, Inc., a start-up company which grew to become a national distributor of pre-employment screening systems, achieving The Inc. 500 List of America's Fastest Growing Private Companies.

Ruth's passion lies in supporting clients to own and cultivate their magnificence.

ruthmdillon@gmail.com
(303) 949-6006

POSITIVITY IS KEY TO EFFECTIVE COACHING
Pamela Lewis

POSITIVITY: THE POWER WITHIN

Incredible strength exists within the mind. When the mind is utilized, it is strong enough to support personal choice in relation to how we respond to challenges and outside influences. When the choice is made to respond to a situation positively, the mind supports the choice.

Imagine waking in the morning to the happy sound of the alarm clock singing out "wake-up, wake-up, and start the day." Every night I do just that. I take a moment to be grateful for my day and then I imagine waking, well rested after a tranquil night's sleep ready for a brand new start to a brilliant day. I have found that when I end my evening with gratitude, visualizing a wonderful start to the morning, my sleep is peaceful and my mornings go smoothly.

For me this is a necessity for I am a night owl who openly admits that mornings can be a challenge. Without creating the intention of having a positive experience in the morning, I tend to hit the snooze button or turn the alarm off completely and remain groggy after I finally wake. With this positive intention I rise, have a glass of water, do a few stretching exercises and I am focused and aware, ready for the day. By creating a positive intention, I choose to have a positive experience in the morning. I respond to the sound of the alarm clock positively because I believe that the sound is ushering in opportunity. My perception of morning changed to a positive one by choice.

Every moment of everyday provides the opportunity to make the choice to be positive. When we choose to be aware of our surroundings, our words, what we allow to influence our mind and create the thoughts that we have, we are capable of making a conscious choice to be positive.

Driving in traffic provides an excellent example of how choosing to respond positively works in everyday situations. What is the average response to a red light? If the light is perceived to be an interruption or obstacle, the reaction is probably negative. If the red light is perceived to be a mechanism of protection that creates order in traffic flow and keeps drivers safe, the response to a red light will be a positive one. What is the average response to the behavior of other drivers on the road? If the drivers are perceived to be poor or in the way, the reaction will be a negative one, perhaps accompanied by language that is negative. If the drivers are perceived to be other people responding and reacting to the world in the best way they can, the response can be a positive one.

Not that long ago I choose to yell at other drivers or felt the disappointment when a light turned red. For the most part, the anger was short lived and I thought that I had let it go by the time I reached my destination. I found myself commenting about the ride to others, recalling specific incidents and details of other drivers. For me, reacting negatively to traffic had a negative effect on my day. I carried the incidents with me and the negativity seemed to create more negativity.

Now, I pay more attention to my behavior than other drivers. Instead of yelling, I ignore or sometimes sing to traffic when I'm behind the wheel. I strive to keep the words positive and pertinent to the situation. This actually serves to lighten my mood while driving. Now when I arrive at my destination, I am amused at my behavior and have few specifics to talk about when it comes to traffic. I have made the choice to change my behavior and have seen the benefits in the form of a more positive attitude. I have turned drive time into my time by actively choosing to respond positively.

> ### *"I have made the choice to change my behavior and have seen the benefits in the form of a more positive attitude."*

Many books have been written making the case for choosing positivity and our ability to control our thoughts by limiting the negativity from the outside. From Norman Vincent Peale to Jack Canfield hundreds of books and thousands of pages have been dedicated to the subject. One of my favorites is Jon Gordon, positive energy coach, author, and speaker who uses accessible stories to promote positive attitude personally and professionally. Many have praised these authors and others for assisting them in creating successful and more balanced lives through various methods based in positivity. If the power is ours to choose, we can choose to make a continuous and conscious effort to cultivate positivity in our lives.

POSITIVITY IN THE COACHING RELATIONSHIP

Joann, 34, found herself stuck in her career. Her work was unsatisfying and she was unable to move up the ladder. Joann felt stuck and sought out the assistance of a coach. During her first coaching session Joann spoke about being denied opportunities presented to others and about her dedication to the company. She mentioned that she had turned down an opportunity during the early years of her employment because extensive travel was necessary. Actually, extensive travel was necessary for all of the opportunities that provided career advancement with her current employer. Though Joann had no personal adversity to travel, her parents had never traveled extensively and had owned the same home during Joann's entire life.

Human minds utilize a variety of self-preservation tools that create barriers to clear and precise communication. Individuals attach emotional reactions to words, people, even things that we wish to accomplish or obtain. These attachments may be shaped by family, religion, or other training. Negative reactions of others serve to support these attachments, so we adapt and choose to protect ourselves. People can become creatures of self-denial in order to maintain a certain level of comfort with others. Often we use language to protect, project, and deny ourselves and to satisfy others. When we become stuck in our ability to obtain goals and reach a point where our true desires are at odds with our need to adapt to the needs of others, we look for change. Often this is the time when the choice is made to contact a coach.

Clients partner with coaches so that they may achieve their goals. In the client/coach relationship a conduit or bond is created between two people through trust. Coaches have an ethical responsibility to provide a positive experience in an effort to allow clients to create a positive outcome and achieve the goals that they wish to reach. Naturally, the only way a client and coach can work together towards achieving a positive outcome is through clear communication.

Well-trained coaches have cultivated a skill set that utilizes the communication tool Neuro-Linguistic Programming or NLP. Developed by Richard Bandler and Doctor John Grinder in the 1970's, NLP provides information on language that coaches can use to create and maintain positivity during the coaching process. NLP provides insight to better understand the client and what they are communicating in order to provide focus and motivation geared toward the true intentions of the client.

Applying the key concepts of NLP allows the coach insight into the language patterns of a client. For a coach it is important to understand what your client *isn't* saying. Is the client saying everything they mean, or is the client deleting information from statements? Is the client generalizing during communications with their coach? Is the client distorting information? If the client is using these language behaviors or patterns (known as Meta Models in NLP), the client is minimizing awareness and consciously or subconsciously limiting understanding.

"Applying the key concepts of NLP allows the coach insight into the language patterns of a client."

When a client is using limiting language, communication may be vague or presumptive and lacking details. Though Joann wanted to be promoted, she did not know why. Joann was also reluctant to talk about the details of the position that she rejected. By listening to what the client is saying and using probing questions coaches work with the client to identify the goals, issues and obstacles that the client is internally focused on. This method can help identify what a client really wishes to accomplish and establish internal motivation in order to reach goals. Joann wanted recognition of her work and dedication to the company, and a new challenge. She was willing to travel. Joann was not willing to relocate. Establishing the true wants and desires of a client through clarification creates a positive client experience and ensures the coach is prepared to properly partner with the client for the most effective and proactive outcome.

Clients may focus primarily on what they do not wish to achieve or have in their lives. Limiting client focus (known as Meta

Programs in NLP) keeps the client from moving toward what they really want. Joann focused only on her boring work and being stuck in a thankless position. By concentrating only on what she did not want, a Joann became stuck in negative mental mud. Language provides clues to thought, both conscious and subconscious. If a client is using negative language the client is thinking negatively. If a client is focused primarily on what they do not want the client is thinking negatively. Joann perceived her employer, her work and everything surrounding her career in a negative manner and repeatedly spoke of her disappointment at being passed over again and again. Going beyond these negative statements and shifting client focus to what they do want creates positive thoughts and a positive energy flow that will propel clients in the direction of reaching goals. Joann began looking for positions and opportunities within and outside of her current company. She is currently maintaining her current position, while exploring a few different opportunities. Positive focus creates positive results.

> *"Language provides clues to thought, both conscious and subconscious."*

LANGUAGE COMMUNICATES MORE THAN WORD MEANINGS

Words have dictionary meanings and often bring to mind certain images. Words can also have several meanings and be influenced by culture and life experiences. Language includes words that evoke a positive response as well as a negative response. Simply put, words and how we use them are an important part of creating positive and effective communication during the coaching process.

> *"...words and how we use them are an important part of creating positive and effective communication."*

Often we neglect the subtle implications that a word has on a conversation. Behind every word is thought. Perhaps the thought is a conscious one. On the other hand, the thought may be subconscious. Language can communicate the level of confidence that a person possesses and provide clues to the inner workings of the mind and thought processes. Language can be used to build up and to tear down. The language used to communicate between the coach and client impacts the outcomes. Emotional context or subtext is created during communication.

Words and phrases have emotional meanings attached as well as dictionary meanings. Some are hot button words that seem to press on a nerve, resulting in the instant access to powerful negative or positive emotions. Though we cannot know every emotional attachment that a person has to a phrase or word, we can be aware of the reaction a person has by remaining connected during a conversation. A coach can clarify with the client and maintain a level of comfort by noticing changes in voice levels and language, and by asking questions. Awareness creates positivity and strengthens the ability to communicate effectively.

What words do you use to communicate? The Center for Coaching Certification provides lists of words to avoid when communicating. These words are called "Poison Words" and though they are words that most of us use daily, they are words that limit the potential of a positive outcome in the coaching process.

Are you ready for an experiment? Reflect on how you are currently feeling. Now read through the list of poison words below, pausing after each for just a moment:

Try	Could
Don't	Should
Doesn't	Would
Can't	Might
Won't	Always
But	Never
However	Need to

How do you feel after reading the list? If you feel a little more constricted than you did before, you have experienced the negative influence of poison words. By removing these words from our language when communicating with others, we take away the limitations imposed by the meaning of the words and the implied negativity so that we pave the way to communicate clearly.

In counter to the negative poison words, The Center for Coaching Certification also provides a list of "Phenomenal Words" to use in conversation. These words provide clarity and openness in communication and create a positive effect with greater potential for positive results during the coaching process.

Are you ready for another experiment? Once again, reflect on how you are currently feeling. Now read through the list of phenomenal words, pausing after each for just a moment:

Now	Imagine
Because	Brilliant
Easily	Enlighten
Naturally	Focus
Aware	Visualize
Experience	Peaceful
Realize	Tranquil
Expand	Tantalizing
Create	Balance
Opportunity	Calm

Now how do you feel? If you feel uplifted, lighter or even excited, you have experienced the positive effect of phenomenal words. By using these words in conversation you are communicating a clear, positive and uplifting message. Also, the use of these words during coaching promotes the use of positive language to the client.

Perhaps this is an excellent time for a quick check. Ask yourself the following questions:

- Does the language I use prompt a positive or negative response in communication?
- How often do I use poison words when communicating with others?
- How often do I use phenomenal words in my everyday language?
- Does the language I use illicit the desired results when communicating?

If your responses weigh heavily on the side of negativity, choose to change your language habits and experience the impact. Delete the poison words from your vocabulary. Concentrate on inserting the phenomenal words into your vocabulary. Be aware of your language with others professionally and personally. Altering your language habits will build positivity and create clarity in all of your communications.

> *"Be aware of your language..."*

Creating a positive coaching experience begins with language awareness and language use that supports, uplifts, and inspires others. Replacing the limiting language of poison words with phenomenal words creates a positive foundation.

IMPORTANCE OF SELF-CARE

Self-care is an important element that aids all efforts in striving to be effective and positive. For a quick check-up ask yourself the following questions:

- Am I a positive person?
- Do I strive each day to have the most positive overall experience possible?
- If things happen that are not positive, how do those things influence me and my abilities?
- Occasionally an off day in unavoidable; how do I respond?

If you responded negatively to the above, more attention to self-care may be appropriate.

Be proactive when it comes to you. Positivity is a choice, and living that choice depends on what we feed ourselves internally, we each have the responsibility to choose the things that feed our own positivity. In this way we are better prepared to share that positivity with others.

Personally, as a coach, I find that I must double my efforts to maintain positivity in my life so that I may serve my clients in the best possible manner. Reading positive material, listening to positive music and journaling help me remain on track. I make a choice to limit what I watch on television or in the theater in order to better control what influences me daily. I enjoy movies, so I choose to watch movies that make me feel good. I have surrounded myself with wonderful, supportive friends and colleagues that keep me on track. Choosing a healthy lifestyle with good eating habits and exercise keeps my energy up and provides countless positive effects on my life. Also, I choose to interact with groups that provide positive experiences, rest, and relaxation. When I want extra help, I turn to my personal coach for much appreciated support. I have found that the more I tend to the positivity in my life and care for myself, the less negative influences impact me.

> *"...we each have the responsibility to choose the things that feed our own positivity."*

Do all you can to care for you and strive each day to have a positive overall experience. We all benefit from time for ourselves and a break in routine. Think about creating a self-care schedule which includes activities that keep you positive. Then, if something happens that is not positive, you are equipped to respond appropriately and that little bit of a negative experience will easily be managed.

If you are having an off day, take into consideration how you are being affected by the experience. Will you be able to effectively communicate? Will you be able to maintain positivity? Once I attended a sales training session where the trainer distinctively and animatedly insisted that if you are having a bad day in which everything is going wrong, cancel all appointments and spend the day away from others. He insisted that more harm than good was possible in these circumstances. Though I do not remember the name of the trainer, or the circumstances of the training, I remember the message and have occasionally given myself permission to make arrangements for a change in schedule.

Others expect us to care for ourselves. Taking the time to remain balanced is rewarded by respect. We show that we are human and are able to understand the experiences of others. Self-care helps us remain connected with humanity. Ultimately, caring for self creates an opportunity for the most effective and positive coaching experience that we are capable of delivering.

> *"Taking the time to remain balanced is rewarded by respect."*

MAINTAINING POSITIVITY IN ALL CIRCUMSTANCES

Important for building positivity in the coaching experience are personal thoughts and beliefs. Ethically the responsibility rests with the coach to self-monitor thoughts, feelings, and beliefs during the coaching process. Truly effective coaching cannot occur without personal commitment to and belief in the process.

If a coach is using methodology that they do not believe in, the method is hindered. This affects the client experience and outcome. If the method makes no sense to you, find another. If you do not believe in the coaching process, or that the process will work, ultimately the outcome will be negative.

Because positivity matters in coaching effectively, coaches have an ethical responsibility to maintain a high level of professional positivity. Coaching effectively and positively when the entire world seems to be spinning in the opposite direction can be a difficult task. In order to maintain professional positivity, set the foundation with personal positivity. Your view of the world and what is occurring will influence your attitude and ability to remain positive and coach with effectiveness.

> *"...coaches have an ethical responsibility to maintain a high level of professional positivity."*

If the client is negative or uses negative language for expression, shift it in a coaching session. Model positivity and provide the tools for the client to develop their own positivity. Positivity supports success and makes goals more easily obtainable. If a client does not respond to the coaching process, explore whether coaching is appropriate at this time.

Be aware of the signals and be prepared to have this discussion with a client. If the client wishes, provide a reference to a colleague. Sometimes providing the most effective and positive coaching experience means releasing the client so that they may find an appropriate match.

Clients may also have other needs that are outside of a coaching level of expertise. Medical issues can create a negative mindset and are best handled by a physician. Referring clients, when necessary, to other professionals is the ethical response and in the best interest of the client. Forming relationships with other professionals is proactive and creates a level of preparation for these possibilities. Discuss your level of expertise with your client and be prepared to release them. Professionally and efficiently provide the most positive experience that you can as they embark on their personal voyage.

POSITIVITY UNLOCKS THE DOOR TO EFFECTIVE COACHING

Whether a client or coach, positivity is the thread that runs through every aspect of the coaching process and binds the work together. Positive outcomes depend on clear communication between the client and coach throughout the coaching process. Clarity in communications is based on a foundation of positive language choices. Positive language choices create positive thought and positive thought creates the atmosphere in which goals can be obtained through positive action which creates a positive outcome.

> *"...positivity is the thread that runs through every aspect of the coaching process and binds the work together."*

Recently a long time client I'll call George was moving forward in his current coaching process. His goals were set. He knew what he needed to do and was prepared to move forward. Then his focus began to change. After a difficult commute, he started talking about all of the negatives he saw in his current situation. I asked this simple question: "George, what do you want?" He stopped talking for a few moments and then he started to shift focus back to his goals and began speaking of all he wished to achieve and the action steps he was using. He easily changed his daily routine and planned for the activities that would move him toward what he desired. From that point on, George became unstoppable and started enjoying every day in a new way. George embraced positivity in his present, focused on his desires, and began easily achieving his future.

Has any situation created a challenge for you during the coaching process? How was the situation resolved? In this case, George realized that by maintaining positivity during his process he had the ability to move beyond the negatives related to his current circumstances. Those negatives that seemed so big at one moment became smaller during the next because of a change in focus. His personal awareness and knowledge of the importance of focus and positivity allowed him to easily change course. By using the power of his mind and the power of choice, George made the choice to retain control of his thoughts and his outcomes.

Each of us has the ability to choose to use the strength of positivity daily and increase our level of effectiveness with others. By utilizing the power of our minds we have the ability to choose our level of awareness, our level of preparedness and our level of positivity. Remember this the next time a traffic light turns red. Make the choice to respond positively and change your perspective. Now take a moment to concentrate on gratitude and what you are grateful for today. Next, set your intention to have a wonderful day tomorrow and be prepared.

> *"Make the choice to respond positively..."*

 Pamela Lewis is a Certified Professional Coach with over 15 years of business and management experience, and ten years of developing presentational tools and collaborating with clients. Pamela broadened her business over the last seven years to include strategic planning, meeting preparation, and business and life coaching. As a designer across disciplines, Pamela merges her business capabilities and design talent to create business and life design.

Her background has included professional development programs in customer service, team building, relationship development and sales. Pamela has been praised for her ability to listen effectively, understand and meet customer needs, and find root causes. Known to bridge gaps between co-workers and communicate honestly and effectively with customers, Pamela has been called on as an intermediary to resolve conflict.

Pamela holds a Master of Business Administration degree with an emphasis in Organizational Development and Psychology and additionally she earned a Bachelor of Fine Arts degree in Visual Communications. As sole proprietor of Pillar Coaching, Pamela supports her clients in realizing their potential and achieving their goals.

Pamela's passion is helping others.

Pamela J Lewis, MBA
pjlewis124@gmail.com
www.pillarcoaching.com

THE PATH TO COACHING EFFECTIVELY
Cynthia Foster

"One important key to success is self-confidence. An
important key to self-confidence is preparation."
Arthur Ashe

Completing the coaching certification class was like drinking a
large, cold drink on an especially hot day. It was satisfying and at
that moment the best thing in the world. Self-confidence covered
me from head to toe and I was ready to take on anyone who would
give me a chance. Then, doubt started to approach. Questions
about my ability were encircling me like octopus arms. What if I
am not good enough? Whom will I coach? Am I ready? Really,
someone is going to trust *me*? Doubt's suffocating hold was
quickly soaking up my self-confidence. How could I stop the
drain of self-confidence and the vision of coaching success before
even starting my coaching journey? Have you ever experienced
the roller coaster sensation of losing your self-confidence?
Sometimes the loss of self-confidence is due to external influence,
while at other times internal influence is the culprit. It was
imperative I find a way to build up my self-confidence again. The
one way I knew to begin untangling doubt's hold on me was to
deal with the major questions of whom will I coach, am I
qualified, and whether someone is going to trust me.

*"Completing the coaching
certification class was like
drinking a large, cold drink
on an especially hot day."*

A focused decision was an excellent starting point to settle my nervousness and anxiety. The question of whom will I coach led me to think about my possible niche. A niche means "a specialized market" according to the Merriam-Webster online dictionary. I decided after much soul searching my niche is young adults from the ages of 19 to 25 because I am interested in helping this age group achieve their goals. I can relate to this age group and I remember having similar feelings of uncertainty about life and which direction to follow. Why couldn't I have been one of those people who just *knew* what they were going to do and how to make things happen? Possibilities, creativity, and life satisfaction exist for those in this age group who are seeking the well-worn path to goal achievement. I knew I wanted to be the encourager for those in the 19 to 25 age group who mistakenly believed they were getting a late start in life and would not catch up because they didn't do what their peers were doing. What connection do you have to your coaching niche?

> *"Possibilities, creativity, and life satisfaction exist..."*

Settling on a niche led to other questions. How to relate to the niche? Immersion into the niche's culture was unrealistic. Fortunately, the valuable information from coaching training saved the day. One of the fundamentals of coaching is to assist the client in reaching his or her goal. That particular fundamental provided much appreciated direction. I wanted to recognize the types of goals important to my chosen niche. What types of goals are important to your niche? Coaching provides the framework to decide on a path, and is flexible enough to take another path if appropriate. What makes coaching an effective tool for goal accomplishment is the frequent self-evaluation question of "am I progressing (based on my own definition) on my chosen path?"

Even though I knew some of the goals typically important to my niche (friends, relationships, success), I explored further by pulling out a sheet of paper and brainstorming about my chosen niche. As the paper filled up with characteristics and thoughts such as student, career, exploration, fun, and emotions, my confidence increased because seeing some of the characteristics on paper made the niche real and attainable. In addition, while reviewing what was written on the paper about my chosen niche I asked myself *how am I going to know these areas really well to maintain focus?* I thought about the self-evaluation question aspect of coaching and I applied the concept to my question. For example, I wrote 'student' on the brainstorm paper. Some of the questions beneath student were: "What does it mean to be a student?" and "What are some challenges for students?" Because I explored some of the questions about relating to students, I had a starting path. My self-confidence meter was rising because I moved forward from deciding whom will I coach to defining and preparing to coach my niche. Preparation for my niche gave me an outline, a roadmap which would help me stay on course during the coaching relationship. What are your benefits of feeling prepared in a coaching environment?

"What types of goals are important to your niche?"

Within a week of completing coaching certification arrangements were made with a client who was eager to begin the coaching process. For the purpose of this illustration I will call the client Mary. Mary is a focused and dedicated individual in her mid-twenties. Upon graduating high school, Mary said she spent some time having fun and enjoying herself. After two coaching sessions with Mary, her commitment to the coaching process impressed me. Therefore, I was surprised when 10 minutes into our third coaching session Mary apologized and asked if we could reschedule the session for another day. Even though as part of our coaching agreement, Mary had the right to reschedule a session, I was shocked when it happened! *Did this mean our coaching partnership was over? What did I do wrong?* It took everything in me not to let the panic show in my voice as Mary and I scheduled the next coaching session.

After hanging up with Mary, I looked like a deflated balloon. Apprehension and anxiety about my coaching ability were quickly grabbing my attention. Then, just like a light switch being turned on, the brainstorm paper popped into my mind. One of the characteristics I wrote was flexible. I chuckled to myself and immediately felt confidence surging through me just like blood flowing into a numb extremity. Being flexible meant that I had to be open to changes with my chosen niche's schedules. I had to expect the unexpected because a client may not remember a previous commitment or a deadline. The objective is to assist the client in moving towards his or her goal, and to focus on supporting the flow of the process.

Normally when someone reschedules an appointment (for example, haircuts or auto maintenance) it involves an inconvenience for the parties involved. With coaching, a rescheduled appointment so soon into the coaching process created unexpected inner turmoil. The turmoil had to be addressed before moving forward. After working through my belief set for the reasoning behind the rescheduled appointment, I was able to once again be confident about my coaching training and refocus on my reasons for coaching young adults. In hindsight, having this experience early on in my coaching career was a benefit because of what I was to experience a few months later with Mary.

At the time, looking ahead to the next coaching session with Mary, I wondered if the communication between us be awkward because of the break in the coaching process. What I discovered while working through the reasons to remain in coaching after experiencing a setback was that I was coaching myself! I had devoted a lot of time to making my niche my own. Reviewing what had happened and looking at my goal (to be a coach) helped me refocus and take steps to deal with this bump in the road. I realized many young adults reach bumps in the road along the way, and coaching helps with the decisions on how to navigate those bumps. Having the insight about the niche created familiarity and allowed me to recognize the benefits of owning and better understanding my chosen niche.

Three Benefits of Owning Your Coaching Niche:
1. Opportunity to explore the niche at deeper level
2. Maintains focus
3. Increases confidence in your coaching ability

> *"The objective is to assist the client in moving towards his or her goal, and to focus on supporting the flow of the process."*

How to prepare for the next coaching sessions with Mary? Once again my mind searched for an answer. After replaying the 10-minute session with Mary over and over in my mind searching for clues on how to proceed I remembered my coaching training manual. The information on personality styles was a welcome sight. I now had a plan and could prepare for the next coaching session. As I reviewed the information on personality styles I fought anxiety that I did not do a good job of preventing my personality style from influencing how the last coaching session ended with Mary. There are different personality styles and a personality style can determine how a person reacts to a situation. I knew from the coaching sessions I had with Mary that she was a no nonsense type of person. She was focused and did not spend much time talking about anything other than her goal. My personality style is quite different from Mary's. I am comfortable with taking my time and relating with people on an emotional level. Therefore, it was important that I not let my personality style influence my interactions with Mary. The 10-minute session with Mary was my third coaching session with her, and I thought I had a pretty good handle on her personality. I had asked her questions about her life and her feelings about various situations to get an understanding of how to relate. Then, as I perused the personality information, I remembered during my coaching training the word snapshot and its relation to the atmosphere a client brings to a coaching session.

As a coach getting to know a client (Mary), I had to identify when she was emotional versus logical and passive versus aggressive. During my initial conversations with Mary I surmised she was logical based on her agenda for accomplishing her goals. Therefore, as I prepared for the next meeting after the break in coaching sessions I thought the best way to approach the session would be to get back to business. However, my strategy was thrown for a loop when Mary and I spoke a few days later. How could I have better prepared to deal with fluctuating personality changes in a client? The Mary I knew as logical was unexpectedly emotional. I had barely finished asking her how she was when responses came back so quickly I was glad she could not see my mouth hanging open. It took Mary five minutes to answer how she was doing. Mary did not finish any of her sentences and her start-and-stop sentence format was confusing. I let her express herself.

As I listened to her, I remembered my highlighted hand-written notes during my coaching training: coaching is not therapy; if client is not "there" consider possibilities; I thought about rescheduling. I did not expect the amount of quick-thinking required of coaching. *How could I suggest Mary and I reschedule since we had just had a recent reschedule?* What choice did I have? Mary's current behavior was not her normal communication style. Just as I was about to suggest a reschedule Mary interrupted her start-and-stop answers and apologized for her behavior. She explained she was dealing with a personal situation and as she was answering my question, she was at the same time getting a mental picture of herself completing her goals.

Again, I was momentarily speechless. I was thankful for the coaching session guideline in front of me. I saw my note of "stay-on-track" next to Mary's name. In coach training, I learned that people are different at different times. After experiencing that emotional roller coaster ride with Mary, my desire was to explore what caused her to go on that ride. I had to remind myself that the client is in the driver's seat and not me. My personality style is to stop everything and analyze what an individual is feeling (which is counseling instead of coaching). My responsibility is to empower the client.

"...people are different at different times."

I had only coached for a few weeks now, and I did not expect the range of my coach training to manifest so quickly! My expectations were that the client and I would have a few sessions to get to know each other better before the challenges appeared. I thought this stage of coaching would be like walking alongside a river bank. Some curves are expected, but for the most part the water would flow smoothly in one direction. Much to my surprise, what I was experiencing was like being in the middle of a churning sea surrounded by life preservers eagerly waiting for me to put them on.

The life preserver with my knowledge of personality styles and how people are different personalities at different times bobbed towards me. I was able to match Mary's behavior with what I knew about communicating with a client based on the signals from the client. Then, as I put my personality style aside and concentrated on Mary, she shifted again and her "let's get back to work" tone put me back on the previous approach; the coaching session continued.

What I learned from the fourth coaching session with Mary changed my approach to coaching. I could feel doubt starting to surround me again. I reviewed the session in my mind and decided what worked for me was having the coach training information in front of me. I decided to make a guideline about personality styles, language patterns, and communication. I found the information on Neuro-Linguistic Programming (NLP) to be helpful because it meshes how we think, the words we use to express what we think, and the influence of our behavior and experiences into an identifiable way to communicate with people. For example, during my conversation with Mary she was scattered in her communication, and then used words to signal she had shifted back to her previous style. If I did not have the training to look for the words and patterns someone uses while communicating, I would not have understood what she was saying to me. Going forth, I wanted to be prepared with options if a client exhibited different personality behaviors. Being prepared would help serve as a guide in case a client did not know how to get the coaching session back on track. Having a guide to incorporate personality styles and NLP communication was helpful because I had a tool to assist with communicating with the client in a manner that he or she would find respectful. An awareness of personality styles made me realize I did have the answer – I am qualified to coach.

Three Benefits of Owning Knowledge of Personality Styles
1. Puts the coach on alert for client communication changes
2. Makes the coach aware to not let his/her personality style guide the coaching session
3. Helps the coach integrate communication with the personality style

OWNING UNDERSTANDING SUCCESSES AND CHALLENGES

Above all, the objective of the coach is to interact with the client as an individual and not interact with the client based on stereotypes or judgment conclusions. Even though I knew this information it was difficult for me to embrace it. Have you ever been in a situation when your judgment of a situation got in the way of the reality of the situation? I had experienced many highs and lows with Mary and I had to thoroughly evaluate our progress. That is where I made the mistake (which I caught in time!) in the coaching partnership with Mary. As I was reviewing my notes, I realized I was looking for facts that would indicate progress in my opinion. I did not see any.

Based on the challenges I experienced with Mary, I reached the conclusion that this coaching partnership was not going to work and that I was wasting Mary's time. I was planning to relay that to her via my energy and tone. However, a comment by Mary during one of our coaching sessions made me realize I needed to shift my focus from myself and focus on Mary. I realized that when I was reviewing my coaching session notes I was looking for signs that I would define as progress and not what Mary would define as progress. I was evaluating *my* coaching progress instead of *her* coaching progress! The judgment conclusion I erroneously made about the coaching partnership with Mary almost led me to sever a productive coaching partnership.

At this point, Mary and I had invested a few months into our coaching partnership. She scheduled weekly sessions and never missed one. During one critical weekly session Mary shared she did not feel confident about where she was at the moment on her life path. Mary thought she did not have any successes. Immediately, I experienced a eureka moment because I remembered Mary's definitions of success she had shared with me many months ago. Therefore, I went through my notes and reminded her about her past accomplishments. She was so surprised to hear what she had done. Mary kept saying she could not believe she had done a particular thing. As I reminded her of each accomplishment, her tone grew lighter, and she repeatedly said "wow, I did that!"

What I learned from that coaching session was to have a thorough understanding of the client's definition of success. That means staying up-to-date on how the client measures success. As the client experiences challenges and different situations, the measure of success will change. Are you measuring success based on your standards or on the client's standards? This particular coaching session with Mary gave my self-confidence a huge boost. I was so happy that I had reviewed our coaching notes and notated them for progress. Yes, I had marked some events based on my definition of success, but that made it easier to see what was not notated, and that is what helped Mary! This was the turning point in our coaching partnership. I sensed her trust in me was growing. She knew I was listening to her, and at the same time was surprised to learn that I was really hearing her too. From then on, after each coaching session I made it a practice to notate areas of success based on Mary's definition of success. Just making that one change in my preparation for the next coaching session with Mary helped me tremendously with my self-confidence. I felt confident that I was prepared to navigate whatever challenge or success Mary discovered during our session.

> *"...have a thorough understanding of the client's definition of success."*

Just as I was congratulating myself for having a strategy to share Mary's successes, I thought *what am I going to do about her challenges?* As a young adult, Mary's life path vision would often change. She felt excited because of the many choices available to her and at the same she battled the pull to beat herself up for coming late to the party. I trained myself to recognize certain keywords and subjects that quickly shut the communication down. This insight was very helpful to me because I made a conscious effort to pay attention to Mary's tone and her word choice to decide if a topic would create a challenge. The plan for dealing with Mary's challenges at first was a challenge for me. How could I help her recognize a challenge and realize that she had the answer to overcome the challenge? This process involved a lot of trial and error. I had to encourage myself that when I chose an unsuccessful approach to coach Mary on her challenges, she did not end the coaching partnership. Instead, Mary continued to make and keep her weekly appointments. Therefore, my coaching plan to deal with Mary's challenges was fluid because I noticed how the various experiences she shared with me affected her perspective. While preparing for coaching Mary as she faced her challenges involved a lot of preparation work from me (I was still learning), often times the challenge areas would lead to a success area. Granted, Mary would shut down on some challenge areas; for most of the challenge areas she turned them into opportunities for growth. In addition, I realized that having a strategy for supporting Mary as she faced challenges and experienced successes helped me stay focused during the coaching sessions. I adjusted my coaching to Mary. Even if the coaching session went down an unexpected path, I had Mary's last definition of challenge and success in front of me as my guide. My self-confidence was overflowing. What do you do to recognize each client's description of success and challenge?

Three Benefits of Owning Understanding Challenges and Successes

1. Supports facing and overcoming them

2. Helps the client recognize his or her successes

3. Reminds the coach that the client is the best judge about the success of a coaching session

73

Coaching is a rewarding experience. Taking the time to own your niche has numerous benefits, especially in that it increases self-confidence. As my coaching partnership with Mary developed, I answered with certainty the questions of who I will coach, whether I am qualified, and whether someone is going to trust me. Who knew that my partnership with Mary would empower me to overcome my challenges? I learned a lot through this process. It takes a conscious effort to step back and evaluate events based on the client's perspective.

> *"It takes conscious effort to step back and evaluate events based on the client's perspective."*

The client will let you know whether things are moving forward or not. Coaching really is a partnership. Coaching young adults was a good choice for me because I am walking the same path as they are in some ways. I am making my way along a path that has many twists and turns as I progress toward my goal of coaching. I now have a compass. Preparation is the key to unlocking my self-confidence and leading me on the road to coaching success.

> *"Preparation is the key to unlocking my self-confidence and leading me on the road to coaching success."*

 Cynthia Foster is a Certified Professional Coach and freelance writer. Cynthia currently coaches young adults transitioning from high school into post-secondary education or other life paths.

The combination of Cynthia's experiences as a non-traditional university student, and a desire to help young adults made coaching a perfect fit. Cynthia wanted to help young adults make sense out of the often overwhelming choices offered to them about their future endeavors.

New to coaching, Cynthia discovered after the first session with her clients, her concerns about launching a coaching business quickly disappeared. The feedback from the clients convinced Cynthia she had an opportunity to make a positive difference in someone's life.

Cynthia's interest in coaching stems from recognizing she already enjoyed listening to family and friends discuss their life desires and goals. However, in some cases Cynthia wanted to do more than listen. Besides telling the person what to do, Cynthia was not aware of other options to help her family and friends.

The hands-on skills Cynthia learned during her professional coach's training made Cynthia realize that coaching provided the proven successful process of taking listening and dreaming about goals to the next level of accomplishing goals.

In her spare time, Cynthia enjoys gardening and learning Spanish.

cynthiafoster61@gmail.com

BUILDING CREDIBILITY AND SUCCESS
Peggi J. Peaslee

If we're not a little uncomfortable every day, we're not growing. All the good stuff is outside our comfort zone." Jack Canfield

This chapter introduces several ways of achieving your goal to inspire belief and coach others in unlocking their unlimited potential. The ultimate goal is success in your business through building credibility, marketing, and obtaining new clients. Each of these topics is worth exploring more individually; here the focus is how they work together and cross boundaries that lead to a solid foundation for business success.

BUILDING CREDIBILITY

Credibility, according to the Merriam-Webster dictionary, means "the quality or power of inspiring belief." There are many facets of credibility including professional accomplishments, volunteer involvement, knowledge and niche within your target market, client success stories, and various experiences from your life. Everything you do has the power of adding credibility to your coaching business. Share your biography with potential clients; it is your resume. Demonstrate how you continue to focus forward in your own life to compel them to take action. Use testimonials from past or current clients to continuously build credibility in your services that relate to your potential new clients.

"Everything you do has the power of adding credibility to your coaching business."

77

Build credibility with clients through quality coaching. Imagine yourself as a client with a coach and think about what you would expect. Developing a trusting relationship is incredibly important. Your clients must feel comfortable divulging various aspects of their life. Remember that coaching is an investment and clients share depth and breadth of information with their coach. Clients seeing, hearing, and experiencing a high level of professionalism, ethics, and values increases your credibility.

Prepare to work with clients who have diverse learning preferences and who process information differently than you. Actively listen and make note of your clients' communication preferences so you can connect initially using their preferred method. Present your business using all learning styles and forms of communication. For example, if your client is more visual, start by asking him or her to share what he or she sees, then work into what he or she hears and feels. Be aware of your own communication style preferences to ensure you are focused solely on your clients' preferences and not your own. Results are achieved by developing trust, making a connection, and adjusting to communication preferences.

Credibility calls for a clear understanding of your client's expectations of a coach. Consider your target market and what they expect. What are your strengths? What will make you stand out as a coach? As you begin your coaching business, explore and decide on your target market, specialties, website design, marketing materials, and foundational aspects such as your code of ethics. Each of these supports your credibility.

MARKETING

When you are an entrepreneur, you become the professional coach, business person, customer service representative, finance manager, marketer, and yes, a sales person! It is valuable to seek help and guidance from other professionals so you balance the many roles in your business. When you consider your marketing budget, think about the cost and best use of your time.

> *"Results are achieved by developing trust, making a connection, and understanding communication preferences."*

Before starting your marketing campaigns and meeting hundreds of new people, take time to understand how many clients you can effectively coach at one time. (For each hour of coaching plan an hour for running your business.) How many clients do you currently have? Once you have a strategy and clear path, begin taking action and moving forward to reach your goal. Use a coach to partner with you through the process. The experience is rewarding and demonstrates your belief in the effectiveness of using a coach. Coaches benefit from coaches!

Understanding your target market will lead to clearly defining the path for your marketing. Who is your target market and what are the reasons this group is your target market? This is an area that I struggled with when I first became a coach. My first thought was that I didn't need a target market because my experiences are with all ages and a wide diversity of people. Well, I was wrong! The good news is that we learn through our experiences. I was able to detect the flaw in my thinking before I really got started. While developing the content for my web site and describing the services my business Desert Coaching provides, I discovered that without a target market, I was challenged with defining my approach and marketing message. Having a target market simply means identifying the group of people you will seek as clients in a niche where you are especially skilled. You can still provide services outside of your target market area and be successful. The target market you choose will help identify your core strengths and passion – which is where your marketing efforts will be focused. In fact, having a defined target market will boost your credibility and generate success. Each demographic has specific views on work, life, balance, and preferences for interacting. Other considerations for your target market are location, culture, language, and areas of specialty. It is important to be comfortable in your target market so you design messages to reach new clients in a manner that will spark their interest and add value to the opportunity.

After you coach people from your target market, do a self-assessment to be sure you have selected the right niche for your services. In order to generate new business, it is important to be confident in the decisions you have made. If you are not 100% confident in your decisions or aren't sure which direction is best, enlist the help of another coach. This is about your business, your ideas, and your choices. Using a coach for yourself provides an unbiased strategic partner who will work with you to guide the process of exploring and achieving your desires. Building credibility in your target market is an ongoing effort that needs attention, a plan, and passion.

Credibility and marketing work together. How do you build credibility within your target market? Results! Credibility flourishes when testimonies are shared by people in your target market. Successful marketing is supported by real-life stories. Client marketing is influential because as consumers, we all like to know that we are spending money wisely. Past clients become a form of consumer reporting. Consider your own thoughts and how you measure the value of a person or product before making an investment. Potential clients have a desire and right to understand what they are investing in and how they will be able to measure their results. Simply stating that coaching is an investment in an individual's life, although it is true, doesn't make you stand out from the crowd. What makes you the best coach selection?

"Credibility and marketing work together."

One of the approaches I take in my business to determine if there is a good coach and client fit is offer a free introductory session. It's an opportunity for both of us to hear and learn more to make a decision on whether the coaching relationship will be productive and beneficial. Your services are valuable and your credibility in your target market is fragile. If you enter into a coaching relationship that is not an effective match, consider the impact it will have on your business. Every coaching relationship should be open and honest so that it leads to positive results. Be honest with yourself and know your limitations. Provide referrals to other coaches in situations where a conflict of interest may exist or with areas that are outside of your expertise. People appreciate honesty and integrity. As a coach, take a realistic approach with your potential and existing clients. Every client is a testimony to your business and will positively share your services when results have been achieved. Both people in the coaching relationship have accountability and responsibility to be honest with each other. Think of every client as the one who will be writing an article on the front page of a business journal. What will the article say? Are you truly driving results and understanding your target market? Focus forward in your business and consider the various aspects of what you do, how you do it, and how it impacts the future.

> ## *"Both people in the coaching relationship have accountability and responsibility to be honest with each other."*

Think about how you communicate and market your business. We all communicate through body language, words, and actions. Smile when you speak with clients, even when it is over the phone. Your demeanor and attitude are apparent in all situations. When coaching clients, we consider learning styles, communication preferences, words, sounds, and images to inspire the best action plans and outcomes. These are great tools for your marketing materials. Think about your favorite commercial. What is it that makes it your favorite? What are the key words, sounds, and visuals that are used to inspire belief in the product or service? Now, play your coaching commercial in your mind. If you don't have one and your mind is silent, take action! Write your own 30 second commercial. Is it powerful, inspiring, and does it contain phenomenal words that lead to action? Does it emulate the challenges and goals of your potential clients? What is your message?

There are many tools available to market your coaching business. Let's begin by considering your daily interactions. You have a great opportunity each day to introduce yourself as a professional coach simply by using actions to create interest. Keep in mind that being a coach means you allow others to speak and share. If you meet a person that works with projects, you can say something like "I work with many projects too and I bet there are similarities." For every profession, there is a clever way to align your business with the individual to inspire questions and desire for more information. You will then be presented with the opening to say "I'd love to share more about the similarities in our work. Let's set up a call!" This approach demonstrates that you respect the person's time and opens the door of opportunity.

Create a brochure for your coaching business. Although we live in a digital age, there are still many people who appreciate a paper to take home and glance at from time to time until they are ready to take action. This can lead to new clients! An inexpensive way of advertising your business can also be your company name, tagline, and way to contact you on the back or side of your vehicle. Think of all the places you drive and places you park. This is very economical and if your tagline is catchy, you will attract more visitors to your website and business.

Consider renting a table or booth at events or professional gatherings. There are hundreds of events that are cost-effective – locate them, ask to attend, and negotiate if necessary. At these functions, be prepared to greet people and hand out information about your business. Develop some basic questions that you can have potential clients answer on-site to determine if coaching may be a good option for them. Purchase inexpensive trinkets with your company name and tagline that serve as reminders to the people you meet. Again, the only limitation you have is your own mind. If your marketing budget doesn't support purchasing items, be creative in finding methods of reaching people and obtaining their contact information for follow-up. Many events like to have raffle prizes. Consider your pricing schedule and offer free sessions to the lucky winner. Another option is holding a drawing for people who visit your Facebook site and "like" it. These are great ways of collecting business cards and contact information.

Contact local radio stations to see if you can be highlighted on one of the shows. Use every method available to you and move past mental barriers that may exist. By offering a free introductory session and a discount to listeners who call in a specified period, you may be surprised by the willingness from the radio station to interview you as a local business owner.

> *"...the only limitation you have is your own mind."*

Partner with businesses. Do you know some of the larger companies or best places to work in your area? Many of these companies offer services to employees that the company either contributes to or makes available to employees through their own incentives and benefit plans. Make the connection. In addition to direct connections, there are several companies that work with businesses to bring services to employees such as Perks Connect. You can learn about these services through internet searches and participation in business networking groups.

Have you considered offering discounts to current clients for referrals and various forms of testimonials? These can be very attractive to people who want to make the investment in themselves and also want to save money. Structure the program so it will work long term. When considering my business, I already offer a charitable donation so I am mindful of other discounts being offered. As a new coach, to start using my skills and gaining testimonials, I provided a considerable discount for the first three month commitment within a limited time period. Referral discounts work well as long as you plan ahead. Structure the program so the discount is honored after receiving the first month's payment from a new client.

In my business, I donate 10% of my clients' fees to a charity of their choice. This is one of the ways I stand out with my clients. They feel good about helping a worthy cause through investing in their future. The amount of the donation, my company name, and the check going to the organization with a letter helps to build relationships with many charitable organizations. My client also receives a copy of the letter. A week after sending the check, I make a personal call to ensure the funds were received and to set up an introduction. This is a discovery process to learn more about the organization that leads to relationship building and more clients.

Through volunteer organizations, you can assist others and offer some of your services at no cost to help them achieve their mission. This is a great way to be philanthropic and market your coaching business at the same time. It's a win-win experience.

Offer workshops or training sessions. Choose topics of interest to your target market. Create a presentation and hold sessions at the library, local bookstore, or community college. At each session, include information on personalized coaching. These sessions are an affordable way for potential clients to evaluate you as a coach and learn more about the coaching experience. Many will know someone else looking for a coach and word of mouth remains an incredible way to drive business results. People trust their friends, co-workers, and family members' opinions. Present yourself well and follow-up diligently with each potential client.

> *"Present yourself well and follow-up diligently with each potential client."*

For your website and electronic marketing seek help from people who understand how to create and effectively market websites. Investing with a professional who understands website marketing and optimization is key to reaching web searchers. A website is not just something you build and people will come. Market your site through links from other websites and through your professional social media sites like Facebook, LinkedIn, and Twitter. Manage your time efficiently and prioritize work by the most beneficial tasks. Decide how to maintain contact with visitors whether it is through phone calls, email, blogging, or a newsletter. Including a call to action on your website, such as enrolling to receive periodic newsletters, is a great way of collecting contact information to continuously build your business. There are thousands of topics that can be discussed quite easily such as effective communication, active listening, inspirational messages, and information of interest for your target market. Develop the relationship with your visitors by providing information – invest in them.

Do your research. Statistics on social media and your target market are readily available through internet searches and offer insight that you may not have realized. Social media is ever changing so you must periodically conduct refresher research to ensure you are staying up with the digital age. Create different messages to use that either lead to visiting your website, adding a comment, or contacting you directly. Since each social media outlet may attract the same or varied demographics of people, post different messages on each to experiment for results. Walk your talk! When communicating on social media sites, be professional and positive. If you post on your personal Facebook page about your business, ask yourself if the comments and conversations you have are reflective of your coaching business. Would you partner with your company if you read through all the posts? You are the image of your business. Even if people don't respond immediately, your goal is to capture their attention and be viewed as a positive, professional person who focuses forward so visitors will want to continue reading or looking for new updates.

"Walk your talk!"

Achieving results takes time. Commit to an active six month strategy for each activity to ensure you reach enough people and can measure results. Modify your messages along the way and track everything you do to see which options tend to get the most responses or spark the highest level of interest. Take a breath and think about what you want. Remember, this is your business and these are your choices.

"Achieving results takes time."

REACHING NEW CLIENTS

This is such an exciting topic! Think about it. You have your coaching business and a toolbox of options, now you want new clients. Easy...right? (Sigh) Okay, be prepared because when you build credibility and market, your business will flourish to where you want it to be! Offering yourself and your coaching services can be very rewarding; it takes commitment like anything else that is worth doing.

Imagine that you have recently attended a small job fair and have seven new contacts. What do you do with them? Do you create a sense of urgency and contact them right away? Do you consider that these people are seeking new employment or may be unemployed? Know your audience! Remember, they willingly shared their information with you and expressed some level of interest. Call them and connect. Schedule a free introductory session. As you begin to ask questions, actively listen to what they are saying and ask for clarification. At the end of your call or meeting with them, explore whether coaching makes sense for them now. Share some of your other client testimonials and show them the value of investing in their future. Decide whether you can offer a discount if they are unemployed. Be creative with your approach and if the person states that they want to use your services and just aren't ready or don't have the money, see if they would like to participate in group coaching. Sometimes potential clients want to experience a positive feeling or see action plans working before they commit. Provide them the opportunity to see how beneficial your services can be and if at all possible, see if one of your past clients will be willing to share some highlights from his or her coaching experience. There is great power in personal connections!

> *"...when you build credibility and market, your business will flourish to where you want it to be!"*

Remember, the research you do will add credibility to your profession as a coach and demonstrates your commitment and knowledge. Think about how you feel when being approached by a company. What is your first reaction? What are the things the company representative can say or do to open your mind to possibilities? Go through the exercise of comparing positive and negative experiences so that you can be sure you are doing your best to reach the right people at the right time with the right message.

Get yourself out in the community and become actively involved in networking groups. You already have a network of people who have various circles of influence. Engage them in conversation and share information, statistics, and the outcomes of successful coaching relationships. Be confident! Get them interested in learning more by inviting them to ask questions. Set a goal to attend a specific number of events and to leave each with a minimum of three new contacts. Practice at smaller events and develop confidence in your approach.

Attend a job fair and work with some of the vendors. Remember that the people you meet have their own circle of influence and you can reach many more potential clients when you connect with others. Be willing to provide referrals back to other companies who partner with you. Job fairs typically include businesses seeking to hire, placement services, resume services, and so many other potential connections. As you collect contacts, note who they are and any goals or information shared. Make follow-up calls when you are happy and can truly connect with the person you are contacting. Reflect on what you know about the potential client and share a fact or other information to show you remember him or her specifically. Make it personal and unique so the potential client will feel connected and important. Each person is special and it feels good when others notice.

SUMMARY

Building credibility starts with your life experiences and builds with every person you meet and every client you coach. Make each experience productive and positive. Ask past and present clients to provide a testimonial for you and request different formats. Build on your credibility by considering volunteer opportunities and giving back to your community.

Use a variety of marketing tools and keep your creative thoughts documented to continuously build on your marketing strategy. Every person you meet is a potential client! Learn as much as you can about your target market including common challenges, preferences in communication, terminology that is most frequently used, and the demographics of the people you intend to serve. Continue learning about your target market, update your data, and add new success stories to your materials. Write blogs or newsletters and share new facts. Develop new affiliations. Offer training sessions and talk about your services and the benefits. Keep your website up-to-date and draw on the expertise of those whose career is in website design and internet marketing. Select promotion opportunities that fit your business, desire and approach to meeting new people. Take your time and develop your commercial. Remember to consider language patterns as well as individual learning preferences to ensure a positive connection. Make your commercial the one that people remember!

Seek to meet the desires of potential clients. Define who you are as a coach and be solid in your conviction presenting a positive and professional demeanor at all times. Offer to share more information and relate the career you have to what others do. You have the power and ability to meet new people every day. Pace yourself and take your time building trusting business relationships.

Now it is up to you. What are your next action steps? What will you do today to make a positive difference in your business?

> *"You have the power and ability to meet new people every day."*

Peggi has more than 20 years in business environments and worked in a strategic capacity in the fields of Human Resources, Technology, Internet Strategy, and Program Development. She partners with businesses and departments within organizations using an inclusive, team-building approach to strengthen relationships and achieve accountability for success. She is currently the Chief Operating Officer at United Cerebral Palsy of Central Arizona.

She has a Bachelor's in Human Resources Management and an Associate's in Business Management. She is Certified to present Civil Treatment programs through Employment Learning Innovations, Inc. and is Certified as a Professional Life, Business and Executive Coach. She believes that life is a journey and seeks to live a life of continuous learning that leads to new paths, new people and greater fulfillment of her legacy.

Through coaching, Peggi works as a strategic partner with individuals or groups to guide the process of achieving desired success that is measurable. She works collaboratively with her clients to ensure understanding, setting goals and action plans that assist each client in attaining their desired goals. Her company, Desert Coaching, donates 10% of proceeds from each one-on-one client to a charity of their choice.

She enjoys and cherishes spending time with her husband, family, and beagles, exploring Arizona, traveling, volunteering in the community, yoga, and cultural dance.

www.desertcoaching.com
Peggi@desertcoaching.com
480-393-6347

SELLING BY NOT TELLING

Erica Torres-Dudziak

WHAT DOES BEING A COACH HAVE TO DO WITH SELLING?

Zig Zigler stated it best when he said, "selling is nothing more than a transference of feeling." When you passionately believe in what you do and how it can help others, your burning desire to be of service will translate into more and more clients. How effectively you communicate this message, and how it is received by the prospect, will be dependent on how well you understand their personalities so that you build rapport, your personal confidence and belief in yourself, plus their buying motives and commitment to change. In this chapter, I will explore the three key tools that will make the most dramatic change in your earning more clients: Building Rapport, Increasing Confidence, and Commitment to Change.

You thought you got into this business to help people make life-long changes - you're not a sales person, right? Actually, being a successful coach means being a great salesperson! I remember thinking, I got out of sales and I picked coaching as my profession because I just want to help people. I realized early on that selling is a part of everything we do. We sell our children on the reasons for making better food choices and our doctor's office on why we need to be seen tomorrow and not in two weeks after our severe cold symptoms have already subsided. As a coach, you are selling people your tools and techniques, and the process for them to develop thought patterns to make positive changes in their lives. *You are selling* - yourself, your ideas, and the hope that things will change if they have a burning desire for success! If you haven't thought of yourself as a salesperson, I encourage you to take on a different perspective. There are many negative stereotypes about sales people (i.e. being pushy, manipulative, having a lack of concern for others, etc.). For some people this is

93

true. If you got into the field of coaching to really make a tremendous impact on other people's lives, then your characteristics are, quite simply, different. You are influencing people to make great changes in their lives that will lead to professional, nutritional, financial, personal, spiritual, and many other kinds of success! What a rewarding career, right? For people to benefit from an accountability partner, a mastermind alliance, or a sounding board, it starts with helping them understand what you have to offer them that will change their life!

Okay, so assuming we are on the same page that we are all sales people influencing our clients to do better and we are just transferring our feeling of passion over to them, let's start on the first thing that needs to happen in order for them to be open to any of our ideas, knowledge, or perspective in their lives. That is......*rapport*.

> *"...being a successful coach means being a great salesperson!"*

THREE POWERFUL COACHING TOOLS TO EARN CLIENTS

1. BUILDING RAPPORT

Rapport is the ability to connect with others on a level where they begin to have an affinity towards you, which encourages the foundation for trust to develop.

When you are talking with your coaching prospects, you will be able to determine if they are more passive or aggressive. This is important because to be effective in connecting with them, you will want to adjust to their passive or aggressive nature. If the passive prospect does buy from you when you are aggressive, it might occur out of intimidation which then leads to the client either canceling or being distant from you during coaching sessions. For example, if you receive a call from someone who is soft spoken and slower to talk, you do not want to begin the call with high energy, moving things along, and at a fast pace. You will build rapport with them more quickly (even if enthusiasm is bursting from every cell in your body) when you begin at their energy level. Alternatively, if you have a more aggressive prospect, step up to their pace.

Remember, like attracts like. Now, it is important to be yourself and also to be respectful. Starting at their tone and pace will help you with connecting better. By the end of the call, your energy levels will be closer! This is actually a good indication that solid rapport has been established. When you begin the call at different energy levels and end the call at different energy levels, you have failed to make a strong connection with your prospect.

In client-focused coach training you also learn that people tend to be either emotional or logical. Most people buy based on their emotions, so it is important to tap into their feelings even when you find that they are more logical in personality so find a way to connect. For example, I was talking with a lawyer who worked with a very large firm based out of Washington D.C. I was able to identify that she was more logic-focused than emotion-based in our conversation. She was big on details, had already communicated things she had researched, and getting her to talk about something personal was like pulling teeth. Then, we connected on the ages of our children and moved forward. She became much more personable and open during the call. She still wanted to have more information and because we had built rapport, we were able to talk through her concerns and reservations. Building rapport is about finding something you have in common to break the stranger barrier. People only care about what you have to say or offer when they know you care about them. It is difficult to really show genuine care for others if they feel that you don't know them and haven't connected with them on a personal level.

> *"People only care about what you have to say or offer when they know you care about them."*

Be comfortable with questions you can use to connect with prospective coaching clients. Here are some ice breaker questions to get you thinking about what will work for you:

- Where are you from?
- How long have you lived there?
- What line of work are you in?
- What do you like most about your job/career?
- Tell me about your family.
- What are some things you like to do for fun?
- What activities do you enjoy doing outside of work?

Your goal is to find something you connect on (i.e. "Oh, I have a sister who lives in Michigan too"). Be sincere about it and also make sure it is relative to the context of the conversation. They will feel a connection with you when you find some common ground. It is great to know if they are married, in a relationship, have kids, etc. Bring this up subtly during the conversation. Remember, you are trying to understand the big picture of what is going on in their lives so that you see how you can be of service as a coach. Remember the power of connecting with them on a personal level. At one time, I would fall into the trap of thinking it wasn't that important and a time waster; I found out all too quickly that selling a coaching engagement was much more difficult without establishing that initial rapport. You could come across as pushy and aggressive. In addition, some of the strong logic people may resist your attempts to know them more personally; they don't want you crossing that barrier. Even though it might take more time, it is essential if you want to talk them through the value of what you are offering. For some practical application, I encourage you to rehearse rapport building questions with someone you feel comfortable with first. Helping people understand how valuable your services are to them can only be accomplished if they trust what you are telling them, what you do, and more importantly, what you stand for as a coach.

After trust is established, as coaches we help the prospect move towards their goals by having them describe their ideal outcome using VAK (visual, auditory, kinesthetic) language. Using this approach is also a great way to build rapport. Remember, like attracts like. If your potential client has a kinesthetic orientation and has been talking about how she feels about certain situations, you can help her to connect with you by matching her language during your initial call. So when you ask questions, use the same types of words. For example:

- "How does this feel to you?" if they are kinesthetic, "How does this sound to you?" if they are auditory, and "How does this look to you?" if they are visual. Their goals will resonate with them faster and more emphatically when you are speaking their language.
- "Would you feel comfortable exploring with me how coaching has supported other people to reach similar professional goals?" for the kinesthetic person, "Would you like to hear how coaching conversations have supported other professionals with similar goals get results?" for the auditory person, and "Would you like to

see how coaching has provided clear direction for other professionals to get results?" for the visual person.

The clients' successes are dependent on their ability to make long-lasting changes in their life that will lead to positive results. This starts with the rapport you build when they are a prospective client. You will know a connection has been made when you hear genuine laughter, an "oh yeah", "I agree", "uh huh", etc. I was recently being pitched by a sales person who was selling a behavioral index assessment. He was a nice guy who fell short in a couple areas to earn my trust:

1. He didn't build any rapport with me. He tried to connect with me on a professional level and relate his service to my business. Since I didn't feel that he cared at all about me, I just believed that he would say anything about his service to make the sale. There was no trust built.

2. The "uh huh's" were one-sided. He would actually interrupt me when I was finishing my statement to say "uh huh" at least three times. In his defense I believe that he was trying to show that we were on the same page and he understood me; having good listening skills and really listening to someone is different than finishing their sentence with "uh huh, uh huh". It felt like he was really saying, "yeah, I got it; stop talking so I can make my point."

Building rapport is the first step, at the same time to earn clients requires believing in what you are selling and believing in the value. This brings us to the second tool for converting more prospects into coaching clients.

"Building rapport is the first step..."

2. INCREASING CONFIDENCE

What does confidence really mean to you? I thought it meant that I felt strong and good about what I did, who I was, my choices, etc. For so many years, I thought I was confident. I did feel good about those aspects of my life. How come my business wasn't taking off like I expected? Do you believe in what you do and the amount you charge for it? Do you have confidence in what you are offering? If you answered yes and your work load is not plentiful, then I ask you to reconsider. You might be confident in who you are and what you offer; you might not be confident in your pricing. Remember that sales are a transference of a feeling. You MUST be 100% confident in what you are selling and at the price for which you are selling it.

How do you know if you are confident in the value of your services? When you can tell someone what you charge without flinching, squinting, or avoiding the subject, then you have hit your number. I am suggesting that you consciously and subconsciously feel comfortable with the fee you set. There are several ways you can come up with fees that you will feel good about.

1. Research your competition and find out what they charge.
2. Calculate the amount of time one session will take (i.e. preparing, session time, post work, follow up, reminders, etc.) and set an hourly amount to it. For example, you might have a personal hourly fee of $75 which includes your hourly rate + marketing time + marketing costs + administrative duties, etc. That means a one-hour session with a client takes you two hours of work, so you charge $75 an hour or $150 per session. Is this a fair amount to your client? Do you feel good about it? Are you easily articulating the value of this session? Work on this so you come up with a figure that keeps you in the game, you feel

good about, and that you can quote with 100% confidence in your voice.

3. Understand the value of what you provide. In a coaching role you are someone who listens to your client, are 100% committed to their success free of any hidden agendas, offers focus and direction, accountability and motivation, and helps them step towards their goals, reach them and set new ones. The benefits of what you offer include achieving weight goals, promotions, work/life balance, love, etc.

Being confident in your pricing is half the battle; it is also important that you believe in yourself and what you are offering to your client. Where does this come from?

- Training and Continuing Education
- Put Yourself Out There
- Practice What You Preach

Training & Continuing Education

Being competent in what you are doing will both increase your belief in yourself, and it will also help your clients have more confidence in your coaching. Foundational training in coaching is important and learning continues. Successful people are life-long learners. Read additional resources about coaching to fine-tune your skills, and strongly consider taking your coach training to the next level. As you work with clients, continue to learn and grow as a professional so that you provide exceptional service.

> *"Foundational training in coaching is important and learning continues."*

Put Yourself Out There

Paralysis by analysis used to be my greatest downfall. I wanted to know so much about a topic that it prevented progress. I remember when I first became a certified image consultant and thought I had to know everything there was to know about selling before I could effectively sell my services. I had sold for many years in other industries; somehow when I became the provider of the service, it seemed different. I signed up for sales training, read every book on sales I could get my hands on, and read tons of articles on the subject. I was an EXPERT on sales, right? Wrong! In truth, I was just confused! Some of the information I acquired shared consistent messages, then other sources contradicted what the previous experts had recommended. At this point, I was terrified to take a call. It was after I got out there and began taking calls and talking with prospects that my confidence increased; it was definitely trial and error! I learned so much more by just talking with people than I ever did listening to a CD or going through a course. The information I soaked in was helpful and when I put myself out there, I understood the concepts and learned what fit for my personal style.

Practice What You Preach

To believe in what you offer, experience the value of coaching. Have a coach yourself, and utilize the coaching tools. Only ask your clients to do something that you are doing yourself (i.e. affirmations, being responsible for your own thoughts with positive thinking, or expressing words of appreciation throughout the day). This will help your personal development and it will also put you in a position to make improvements because you see first-hand how these techniques can be better used with your clients. Every day I wake up in appreciation of everything that I have. I start my day with gratitude to put me on the frequency of positivity. I see and read my affirmation sentences in my bathroom as I get ready in the morning. I am constantly filling my mind with productive and positive messages by taking advantage of educational CD's during my drive time. I use a technique I learned from Andy Dooley, the brother of one of my favorite motivational authors, Mike Dooley (quoted in "The Secret" by Rhonda Byrnes). During one of his workshops, he shared a great tool to help get past doubt. Sometimes when you read or hear positive affirmations, you don't believe in what it says. It helps to continue hearing it every day over and over to get into the subconscious. I have had clients just stop listening because what they wanted and what they were hearing were too far apart from what they believed was their reality right now. In just a few sentences Andy taught us how to move into belief with: "wouldn't it be nice, that's right, and in the meantime". I found this technique works if you use either or both "wouldn't it be nice", "that's right" and make sure to end it with "in the meantime". For example:

- Wouldn't it be nice if I got 10 opportunities to sell my services each day.
- Wouldn't it be nice if I converted 25-30% of those opportunity calls into clients.
- Wouldn't it be nice if each of those 5 clients signed up for at least 3 months of my coaching services.
- That's right, I have 40 clients that I work with on a consistent basis.
- That's right, I am making over 10k a month doing what I love.

You can use each of these phrases until you really start to feel good. Now you are in the zone of being pumped up; in reality you don't have any or maybe just a few clients. To avoid feeling down, you can remain excited by bridging this gap using "in the meantime".

102

- In the meantime, I am focusing on my marketing strategy so that the number of calls I get per day increases.
- In the meantime, I am practicing the sales process of expressing the value of my services with my colleagues and trusted friends so that I will be confident when I receive the calls.

Believing in what you are saying is key to confidence. Be truthful with yourself if you expect to feel confident, and do dream bigger than your current reality in order to reach your goals.

> *"Believing in what you are saying is key to confidence. "*

Now that you believe in what you are selling and the value at which you are selling it, and you have built a connection with your prospect, it is time for us to explore the third tool required before asking your prospect if they would be interested in a coaching relationship and commitment to change.

3. COMMITMENT TO CHANGE

For a coaching relationship to have value, the prospective client must have a commitment to change. Before you can identify or help them to see their commitment to change, it may make sense to explore how a lack of commitment to change and to move towards their personal goals has a negative impact on their life. Your potential clients are calling you because they are looking for a positive outcome or change in their life, which means they have been less successful doing it alone or sometimes because it has caused some unwanted things to transpire in their lives. For example, excess weight and lowered self-esteem can be the result of your prospects not having the focus, motivation, and follow through a coach offers. Ongoing stress and anxiety, with a reduction in overall mood and well-being, can be the result of an executive not meeting their expectations for themselves in the workplace. Digging in and exploring their efforts and lack of results is critical to helping them understand why working with you is so important for their success. If you don't have a good understanding of their goals and what has prevented them from being successful in achieving them, then you don't really have a handle on what they are seeking. People seek coaches when they realize they are experiencing pain, or lacking personal or professional satisfaction (i.e. passed over for a promotion, struggling with identifying a career path, marital strain, depression from addictive eating patterns, etc.). Some examples of questions to understand the impact of their current behavior are:

1. How has the conflict between you and your coworkers affected your work? Your productivity? Your health?
2. How has your weight gain had an impact on your self-esteem? Your relationships?
3. How has your lack of focus affected your business and/or profit margins?

A quick caveat here: be careful under the context in which to ask these questions! Make sure the prospective client has expressed a parallel of the issue to their pain before making an assumption or probing with more questions. For example, if a work conflict has not had a negative impact on their work productivity or health, you wouldn't want to ask the question in number one.

Once you have uncovered the unwanted pain in their life from not having reached their goals, you can move them towards a place of hope by having them paint a picture of what they will see after working with you and moving toward their dreams. Painting a picture is a pretty classic sales technique, and as a coach you make this even more powerful by helping your prospective client to use auditory and kinesthetic language too. This makes reaching their goals even more real. If the prospect's goal is to meet his ideal love match, and his pain is not having someone to share memorable activities with, paint the picture by having him share how he would see himself in a mutually satisfying relationship with someone who has many common interests with him. You would then have your prospect expand this vision by stating what they would hear that person saying on a date or at the end of the day, and then also describe how it would feel to have this special person in their life. Of course, you would want to begin with their VAK language preference first and even reiterate the preferred language style at the end. Here are ways of moving the prospect in the first example question above from pain into hope:

1. What kind of relationships would you like to experience with your coworkers?
2. What will your work environment sound like when everyone treats each other with respect?
3. What will productivity look like for you when the culture of your work environment is encouraging?

What are some pain to hope questions you can use with the second client dealing with weight gain and self-esteem?

_____

_____

_____

_____

What are some pain-to-hope questions you can generate for the third client who was dealing with focus issues at work?

_____

_____

_____

Once you have moved them toward hope, explore the prospective client's commitment level to make a change. Before talking with you, they might have thought their commitment to change was a six out of ten. After they have been able to communicate what these issues have caused in their life and what they want to see happen, ideally they have an upward shift in commitment.

Here are some example questions to determine their commitment level:
- When are you looking to implement changes?
- How quickly will you start?
- What are some barriers to making these changes happen?
- What time are you willing to commit to reach these goals?

What are some other questions you can list?

_____

_____

_____

"...explore the prospective client's commitment level to make change."

PUTTING ALL THIS IN TO PRACTICE

Turning a call from someone who had a few questions to beginning the foundation of a great coaching relationship can be a very rewarding experience. Remember the Three Powerful Coaching Tools during your conversation and your conversion from prospects to clients will increase exponentially!

Building rapport will help you get to know your prospective client and their wants. It will allow them to get to know and trust you as they consider you for their coaching partner. Trust is built with rapport and strengthened when they can hear the passion in your voice and how much you believe *you* can help *them!* Believing in what you do comes across to your prospects and you want to leave them with hope because with your support, they can reach their goals! People buy more on their emotional investment, so it is important to help them understand during the initial call what this lack of strength in their life has cost them personally and professionally. They know they are not at their highest level of success or they wouldn't be calling. Shift prospects into fully describing their ideal and exploring their reasons for committing to make it happen.

What are two things you will do this week to convert prospects into coaching clients?

1. _____
2. _____

Aside from an increase in number of clients, what are some other ways you can measure your progress? Some suggestions to get you started are to increase the number of specific follow-up day/times to call prospects back, establishing rapport and listening so your prospect opens up more during the initial call, and feeling a genuine connection.

1. _____
2. _____
3. _____
4. _____

It is my hope that these three tools will help you take a different perspective on your business and ultimately, take it to the next level. To your success!

"To your success!"

Erica Torres-Dudziak, AICI FLC, is a Certified Professional Coach through the Center for Coaching Certification, and a recognized image consultant through the Association of Image Consultants International. She founded Positive Perceptions, LLC in 2007, a personal and professional development resource that helps women feel more fulfilled and balanced in their career and personal life by reaching their next level of success in the workplace, their health, and at home.

Erica is passionate about helping people achieve their goals by staying authentic to themselves and maintaining a healthy work and life balance. She has over 11 years of sales experience including positions involving one-time closes, employee recruitment, health & wellness consulting, and selling her own coaching, workshops/trainings, and image consulting services. Some of her clients or partners have ranged from and/or worked for the Federal Reserve, NASA Glenn Research Center, Case Western University, Oberlin College, Red Cross, Association of Administrative Professionals, Hotze Health & Wellness Center, and SS&G.

Erica@positiveperceptions.info
(440) 258-5384

108

PRESENT YOUR WAY TO PROFITS
Megan Huber

"There are three things to aim at in public speaking: first, to get
into your subject, then to get your subject into yourself, and lastly,
to get your subject into the heart of your audience."
Alexander Gregg

BENEFITS OF SPEAKING

You've earned a coaching certification, established yourself as a
business, set up an account at the bank, your website is live, and
your home office is organized. You built it, now they will come –
right? Well, they'll come alright, when you *ASK*. Very few
people who start a coaching business are also marketing and sales
gurus, and many coaches shy away from asking for business. It is
imperative for any business to build the marketing and sales skill
set necessary to thrive and experience continued growth. Upon
opening your doors for business, the next, and probably most
important step, is to decide on how you will market yourself as an
expert in your industry so that you start generating an income. It
is best to select one to three marketing avenues to focus on for at
least three to six months. As a coach, one of the best forms of
marketing is through speaking. When I started my business, my
main marketing tool was speaking. My initial goal was to speak
twice a month; by the fifth month I was in business and I was
speaking up to ten times per month.

Many survey and research results show that most people would
prefer death over speaking in public. As a result, a coach who
speaks in public has the ability to demonstrate to an audience that
they are smarter than other coaches who aren't speaking in public.
Afraid you'll drop dead in front of a crowded board room? Move
forward. First, begin by referring to yourself as a speaker and
position yourself as an expert. Call yourself a speaker in your e-

mail signature line, on your business card, on your website, at your talks, and when you introduce yourself at networking events. People will immediately take note and think of opportunities where they might need a guest speaker for a monthly meeting at the office or at their weekly networking event. By referring to yourself as a speaker at networking events, you give yourself the opportunity to ask for speaking referrals from other networkers.

Speaking to large or even small groups puts you in front of more people at once. Imagine how long it would take to build your private coaching clientele if you only provided complimentary sessions versus giving five talks a month to groups of ten or more people? Of course only some of the people in the room at your talks will want to invest in private coaching. After all, private coaching is a significant financial investment, and it's also an investment of someone's time, effort, and energy. Some people are just not ready to take that next step. A few audience members at your talks will be ready to invest in taking their business to the next level.

Be ready to offer something. Perhaps you offer the audience tickets to a series of three or five virtual workshops that you will conduct instead of offering your most expensive and time consuming coaching package. When I first started speaking, I had no offer. I got no business from that plan. Then, I started offering a coaching package. Still didn't get much business because people only saw dollar signs. Once I developed additional products and services, I saw my clients and income rapidly increase. While I was perfecting my offering, I was also realizing that only some people are a potential client.

Identify your potential client. I spent time making sure I was very clear with myself on who I wanted to help and how I wanted to help them. Put another way, it was imperative that I have a target market and a niche within that market. When you do hit the right

111

group with the right message, it allows participants to self-select themselves.

As a coach, you want to work with people who are ready and willing to invest in themselves personally or professionally, and grow to the next level. Allowing people to pick you is like an ace in the hole.

> *"Allowing people to pick you is like an ace in the hole."*

GETTING BOOKED

You've decided that your top marketing priority is going to be public speaking around your local community. This next step is where most coaches get stuck. Where do you speak and how do you get booked? It's actually easier than you think! Remember, most people would prefer death over public speaking, so local businesses doors aren't getting knocked down with speakers inviting themselves in to give a talk. So, how do you decide how many talks to give and what product or service to offer? Keep in mind that when starting out in the coaching industry, no one knows you yet, so expect to pay your dues before you get paid big bucks to be a keynote or guest speaker. Expect to speak for free and make it an opportunity to get comfortable converting audience members into paying clients.

First, at the beginning of each month, decide how much money you want to earn through speaking. This can be accomplished through a simple formula. Simply plug in the numbers that work for you and your level of commitment to speaking as a way to market your business. Then multiply the percentage who will buy by the price of your offer to estimate earnings. In the coaching industry, a great conversion rate is around 20%, so I'll use that just to be safe.

# of talks given X avg. attendance X 20% X offer price = earnings

Here's an example. For the month of June, I am giving 10 talks with an average attendance of 10 people. At the end of each talk I am offering a workshop for $197. When multiplied together, my monthly commissions from speaking for the month is $3,940. If I prefer to make more than that total, I can choose to conduct more talks, make sure I am talking to larger groups, convert more people into becoming a client, or offer a more expensive product or service. By using the formula, you have more clarity and direction when booking yourself for speaking engagements.

Next, get on the phone and start booking! Not sure who to call or where to talk? Here's an idea. Start locally and think globally. Get in your car and drive a comfortable distance in each direction. Write down the businesses or organizations where more than one person works. Find out who and how to contact each place on your list. Figure out if you have a mutual connection with the decision makers on your list and write those down, too.

Why would any of these places want you to come speak? Well, they won't until you ask!

WINNING IT

Most business owners or speaker coordinators have a problem that they want solved such as procrastination, lack of focus and clarity, or a low client base. Be sure to state how your program is relevant to the problems they are facing. Indicate that you have a solution people will be excited about hearing and then implementing in their business. One area of concern for business owners and managers is that guest speakers will be boring and simply come in with an hour long sales pitch. Reassure them that your talk will be educational, interactive and engaging, fun and different. When it's time to get your program on their calendar, position yourself as being in high demand. Let them know that you are busy and you are willing to make time for their business or organization because you know what you offer is valuable to the success of the audience members and the organization they represent.

> ## *"Most business owners or speaker coordinators have a problem that they want solved."*

It's time to move past hiding behind your e-mail account and start moving forward with confidence and initiative. Get out a sheet of paper and draft a script that's designed to get you booked for speaking. Use a confident tone when the phone is answered. Ask for the decision maker by name and state who you are and what you are giving them. The name of a mutual connection can build your credibility and is a winning tool to use when booking. Once you have the decision maker on the phone, show your expert status by stating the organizations and businesses you've spoken to and what you talked about. Let them know that your program was well received by participants.

At the end of the call make sure you have a simple system for what will happen next. Confirm the time and date, send them your speaker one sheet for promotional purposes, direct them to your website, and provide your phone number. Indicate that you'll be touching base the week before the talk to make sure everything is in place.

LOSING IT

Knowing what not to do is just as important as knowing what to do when booking yourself for speaking engagements. You know you're losing the battle when you sound like a telemarketer. Remember, you want to exude confidence and sound like you've done this a time or two before. When you allow negative self-talk to block your brain, it's very easy to convince yourself that you are bothering people. Not true! Most people welcome guest speakers as long as they bring a solution to a problem that they are facing (and everyone has problems).

A calendar that appears to be wide open will make the person on the other end of the line wonder why you have so much free time and they may hesitate to bring you in. Make sure you get booked while you are on the phone. Meeting for coffee or lunch to discuss whether or not you'd be a good fit means your calendar is too wide open. You already know that you are a good fit. Sending e-mails will not get you booked unless you have a very strong, personal relationship with the decision maker so call unless you are completely confident that an e-mail will close the deal.

> *"Knowing what not to do is just as important as knowing what to do when booking yourself for speaking engagements."*

Does it seem like this is a bit out of order – getting booked then developing the talk? Why would anyone be confident enough to book themselves if they don't already have a signature talk? The organization you book yourself with will never know! The first step is deciding that you are going to speak as one of your top marketing avenues. Hopefully, you already know your area of expertise, so coming up with a topic to talk about is really pretty effortless. Remember that when you book yourself, you aren't going into great detail about the talk itself, just the problem that you can come in and solve. Actually, it gives you the opportunity to tailor your talk to your audience. I am confident that once you get your first booking, you'll work tirelessly to ensure you put on a good program that they talk about positively!

> "The first step is deciding that you are going to speak as one of your top marketing avenues."

When developing your signature talk, ask yourself the following questions:

- What is my end result?
- What will the audience think?
- What will the audience feel?
- What will the audience believe?

If you're not sure what title to give your talk, take some time to think about and write down the problems people say they have, especially if you already have a few private clients. What are you helping them with? What are their biggest obstacles? What do they want? Tailor your talk titles based on the consistent problems that you are seeing and hearing.

While developing your signature talk, it is important to remember that you want to convert audience members into paying clients. They don't have to be private clients – they could be workshop attendees, or maybe they will buy an audio set of your signature system that you have on sale. Let's take a moment to outline the order in which to develop your talk, and the pertinent information to include that will set you apart from the pack of coaches in your local market.

INTRODUCTION

Use the introduction to confidently state who you are, who you help, and how you help. This is known as an expert statement. Indicate the problem you are seeing and the transformation that could potentially take place. People love stories and relate better to other individuals when they humanize themselves and share personal stories to which the audience can easily relate. Share your personal story or experience with the problem you just stated. Next, get the audience to focus in and listen by getting them to identify that they, too, are facing the problem that you are about to help them solve.

Here's the short version of my introduction: My name is Megan Huber and I help small business owners and entrepreneurs reach their goals faster and easier. The #1 reason why most businesses lack growth is because they fail to take the time to write goals and a plan to achieve those goals. I do this through private coaching, group coaching, workshops, teleseminars, and programs just like this one today. The problem that I'm seeing is twofold. First, business owners aren't clear on where they want to go and how to get there – they simply aren't writing down their goals and a plan to achieve those goals. Second, I am also seeing a lack of follow through. We say we're going to do something and we start, then we don't finish. I was there, too, just a short time ago. I wasn't clear on my purpose, I was afraid to pick up the phone, I procrastinated, and had a lack of confidence. I knew that I had the potential to change lives while growing my business, so I hired a coach, got a mentor, started reading books from experts in the industry, and attended a couple of key conferences. I learned about the mistakes that others had made so that I wouldn't have to make those same mistakes. By a show of hands, how many of you write down your goals and a plan to reach those goals each month, each week, and each day? (Usually no one raises their hand, so they immediately know there is room for improvement.)

TRANSITION

After you've spent a few short minutes setting yourself up as an expert who once felt the same pain as your audience, it's time to transition into the main points of the talk. Rather than jumping right in to the first main point, guide them forward with a shocking exercise or statistic. Since I talk about goal setting and planning, I share a brief article about a study conducted with Harvard MBA students which proved that graduates who had written goals and a plan to achieve those goals made more money than all of those who didn't combined. Immediately, people are sitting on the edge of their seats because they all just admitted that they don't write down their goals or a plan to achieve those goals either! Now they are ready to listen and take copious notes!

> *"...guide them forward with a shocking exercise or statistic."*

Main Points

When most speakers give a free talk, they tend to make one of two major mistakes: wing it or teach too much. If you wing it, your audience will immediately call your bluff. Preparation is a must for anyone to reach success in a chosen path. Spend some quality time developing your talk, especially the introduction and the close because they are ultimately the most important parts. Most coaches think that the main points are the most important, that the main points will do the selling. In actuality, the coach is doing the selling with the opening and the close at the end too; what was shared in the middle helps and it demonstrates credibility. It isn't necessary to solve all of the audience member's problems in your talk. Remember, you want them to come to you at the end knowing you are worth paying for a way to solve their problems. If you give away too much information, they will feel as though they don't need you anymore because they can now move forward and be more successful on their own.

Remember that you ultimately want business from the talk, so you want to give the audience enough to make them feel like they have a problem that will require your help to solve. Share a set of myths that aren't true or common misconceptions. Stick with providing three to five main points. For example, share a problem and three to five ways to solve that problem. Provide three key strategies or five secrets to success, ideas to earn money in a tough economy, or marketing strategies to increase profits. Whatever your main points might be, tell them what, and then let them know that your offer is the how. People purchase on emotion, so sharing stories and examples is very powerful. At the end audience members must feel as though they will benefit from what you offer to ultimately turn things around for their life or business.

> *"...share a problem and three to five ways to solve that problem."*

NEXT STEP

You're now nearing the end of your talk, the second most important part of the program. Up to this point, you've covered quite a bit of information, so it's important to include a quick review as a way to remind the audience that they have a problem and that you can help. After all, you are now the expert since you, too, have lived and survived to tell your story. Indicate to the audience what will happen if they walk out of the room with the same problems. Nothing will change! They will continue to spin their wheels and repeat the same actions expecting different results. People don't like to make decisions, so make this an easy one for them by telling them what they need for a full transformation. You are their knight in shining armor and it just so happens that you have a product or service that will do the trick they've been looking for to experience growth and success.

CALL TO ACTION AND CLOSE

In addition to your initial introduction and first few words as a roomful of eyes stare at you, the call to action and close is the most anticipated and it is also the most important. If there is one thing that you learn from this chapter, I hope you learn that you will never attract business. You must *ASK* for business. You might attract people to attend your free talk; unless you *ASK* them to buy a ticket to your workshop or check the box on your handout for private coaching, they hesitate. Not because they don't want to, simply because you didn't *ASK*. Prompt them to do something next. Your website might attract traffic; unless you have a call to action in a very visible location, you will lose one opportunity after another to build your list and put yourself repeatedly in front of the same person until they decide to work with you as a coach. By not asking, you immediately devalue your product or service, and you also do a major disservice to the people who can truly benefit from what you have to offer.

The call to action must be treated as part of your talk just like the introduction and each main point. Coaches tend to tense up and second guess their value at the close and it ends up either being completely forgotten and skipped, or it comes out with a voice full of cracks and squeaks. Prior to this point in your talk, select a few key areas to begin seeding your offer to the audience. For example, after your first main point, simply say that the topic will be elaborated upon in great detail at your upcoming workshop. Get the audience thinking that they want to know that information so when it's time for your close they already know that they want more and are ready to take action on your offer.

I mentioned earlier that people don't like to make decisions and they certainly don't like to be given too many choices to select from. Make your offer clear and to the point. Of course, in your coaching business you probably offer multiple products and services; at the end of the talk you're going to offer them *ONE* next step. I like to call this step your entry level program. Most people are not going to invest in your $5,000, 6 month group coaching circle after hearing you give a 30 minute talk. They don't know, like, and trust you quite that much yet. They might be willing to purchase your 5 CD audio set for $97 or sign up for your workshop for $247 which provides the information to take their business or life to the next level. To make it even easier, give them the option to pay in full or pay in installments. Better yet, make a money back guarantee or drop the price if they register on the spot! Make them an offer that is hard to resist.

121

"...at the end of the talk, you're going to offer them ONE next step."

When developing your call to action on paper, think back to the many times you have made a purchase. What triggered you to spend your money? Obviously, you spent money on something that you felt you needed or wanted. You also believed that it would help you, you clearly understood what you were buying, and you had an urgency to make the purchase on the spot. The minute an audience member walks out of the room, the chances they will ever purchase from you in the future go way down. For the few that will, collect their contact information by giving away a free report that you'll send everyone the next day, or provide a give-away for a free strategy session, or access to a short audio CD from the last tele-series that you recorded!

Now, you may be wondering, "What if the organization I speak for doesn't want me to do a sales pitch?" That's an easy one to tackle. When you shared your main points, hopefully you had the audience members take notes on a handout that you provided them. Include an order form for your offer on the handout. When you reach the call to action, you've removed the pressure from yourself and the audience. By including the order form on the handout, you can show them exactly what to do next if they are ready to move forward. If you want to get something from everyone, you can also include space on the handout for testimonials and referrals. All isn't lost if not everyone takes you up on your offer. Perhaps you are provided with a handful of names and contact numbers for future bookings! Ideally, you want everyone to feel comfortable at the end of the talk, so simply invite those who are ready to move forward to meet you in the back of the room with their questions and order forms – be sure to get them pumped up!

Ultimately, at the end of the day, the marketing tools you select are used to help you earn a living. Friends and family members might not understand how in the world you can earn a living through speaking. Surround yourself with other coaches who are out there doing the same thing. Find or start a group coaching circle where an expert coach is leading the group on speaking to sell. Share your successes and failures with people who are in the trenches with you. If your marketing budget is low or even non-existent like mine was when I started coaching, remember that speaking is totally free. It might be scary – remember that everyone in that room is rooting for you to do well. They want you to provide them with a brilliant message so that they, too, can make a big difference in their own lives and the lives of the people that they serve.

> "It's not who you are that holds you back,
> it's who you think you're not."
> *Anonymous*

"They want you to provide them with a brilliant message so that they, too, can make a big difference in their own lives and the lives of the people that they serve."

Upon partnering with Megan in a professional coaching relationship, expect to experience fresh perspectives on personal challenges and opportunities, enhanced thinking and decision making skills, enhanced interpersonal effectiveness, and increased confidence in carrying out your chosen work and life roles.

Megan attended UNC-Wilmington and earned her Bachelor of Science degree in Business Administration with a concentration in Management and earned her Master of Arts in Teaching from East Carolina University. Megan's career began as a high school business teacher where she acted as advisor for student organizations, served as the Tennis Coach, and Football Athletic Trainer as well as coordinated the Graduation Project. Megan has also taught online for North Carolina Virtual Public Schools for four years where she served as Course Lead.

Megan began her journey into entrepreneurship by starting an international marketing business. She expanded her skills in growing and leading her team of business partners by earning her Certified Professional Coach Certification. Through this experience she discovered her true passion and purpose lies in teaching and coaching entrepreneurs to tap into their full potential and create a life of their dreams. Megan speaks to groups including the Chamber of Commerce, Economic Development Corporation, networking groups, and multiple direct sales teams. She has served as a national speaker and trainer for Essential Bodywear, LLC and Shaklee Corporation. Megan is an active member of the Junior League of Durham and Orange Counties and the Chapel Hill Chamber of Commerce.

www.reachteachinspire.com
919-906-0753

I'M A GREAT PERSON – I THINK
Nicole Stragalas

Have you come across managers who seem to be a strange mix of self-confidence and insecurity? People who are very defensive about work incidents that don't seem to warrant such intense responses? Or people who talk a good game about their skills and then sometimes act like they're uncertain about whom they really are and their value? It's tempting to attribute these behaviors to quirks of personality or perhaps link them to self-sabotage. Often it is related to their self-esteem.

Based largely on the work of Michael Kernis, with the support of other researchers, we've learned that self-esteem can be described with more specificity than high or low. Kernis' research reveals high esteem can be stable/secure or unstable/fragile, and low self-esteem can also break into these classifications. We've also found out, through the studies of Deci and Ryan, that self-esteem can be contingent or based primarily upon performance outcomes for some people in areas such as academics, work, physical attractiveness, or acceptance in social circles.

It's often assumed that managers and leaders are self-confident individuals with moderately high to very high self-esteem. In American culture, the image of a corporate executive is a person who is self-assured, somewhat outspoken, and unaffected by the day-to-day ups and downs of business life. Think about public figures and their image that you are familiar with in leadership roles.

In executive coaching, we see beneath the public exterior, asking our clients to share experiences that reveal their decision-making and motivation processes. We also listen to their stories and learn clues that help us recognize the state of their self-esteem based on examples of selected behaviors. As coaches, we begin to

126

distinguish between the externally presented confidence and actual self-perceptions related to self-worth and authenticity.

> ## *"In executive coaching, we see beneath the public exterior..."*

WHAT MAKES RECOGNITION OF THE STATE OF SELF-ESTEEM IMPORTANT?

Kernis and his team were showed that people with fragile high self-esteem behave differently than individuals with optimal and stable high self-esteem. When self-esteem is fragile, people do not gain the same psychological benefits and life outcomes associated with secure self-esteem. Most important, people can learn new thought processes and patterns generating authentic high self-worth, gradually shifting from fragile to optimal self-esteem.

Although the improvement of self-esteem may seem to be outside of executive coaching, an understanding of behavioral cues and support for a shift in thinking remain within the bounds of management development. Many of the detrimental actions that lead an executive to require constructive coaching could be linked to fragile high self-esteem. It is valuable to recognize the signs and establish an action plan that addresses directly relevant aspects of the individual's work and interpersonal relationships.

There are direct as well as implicit costs incurred by the organization when a manager with unstable high self-esteem feels threatened in some way and attempts to address the perceived dangers. I observed with one client company a literal path of destruction generated by one senior executive, a person I nicknamed the *Tasmanian Devil*. Just like the cartoon character, this individual would whirl through a group of people and projects, chewing up everything in sight. The executive had an inconsistent history—many successes, and many complaints of corrosive behavior and arrogance that affected morale and employee engagement. Financial successes had been obtained; it was often through process control, as productivity was uneven in the managed departments.

A very senior level promotion opportunity became available, and this person was placed under consideration for the role. During the interview process, this individual took several steps that were perceived by the hiring committee to be self-sabotage. A number of people in the committee expressed serious misgivings; ultimately the *Tasmanian Devil* was chosen for the role—with the caveat the person would work with *two* coaches.

In less than twelve months, the promoted executive dismantled entire teams, shifted senior leaders out of long-established groups, fired or transitioned out a substantive number of middle and front-line managers, and pushed to change and control programs deep into the levels of the business unit. The *Tasmanian Devil* openly joked about his two coaches, clearly insulted by the implications and flaunting the coaching in meetings and large group conferences. Financial results and production results were not realized. Sizable numbers of talented individuals who were afraid of career derailments left the business unit and even the company itself. After 14 months total, the executive leveraged his title to take a similar role at another company altogether. That next role lasted approximately one year before the executive moved on to a third company.

This case study reveals some of the key behaviors and outcomes associated with fragile high self-esteem. Without coaching and an individual's conscious modification of behaviors, issues with aggression, hostility, and self-sabotage can surface. Unchecked, these issues lead to decreased morale, lower retention, disruptions to succession planning with high potentials, and loss of business productivity and revenues. Equally important, the company ends up with an executive who must be managed out of the organization.

Most individuals with unstable or fragile high self-esteem are not as extreme as the *Tasmanian Devil*. That executive did not wish to address shortcomings or take ownership of the problems related to behaviors. Coaching this individual would not alter the outcome because the person actively refused to participate in the process. It is possible, through this example, to appreciate the significant impact fragile high self-esteem may have and begin to recognize the characteristics associated with these managers.

IDENTIFYING CHARACTERISTICS ASSOCIATED WITH UNSTABLE / FRAGILE HIGH SELF-ESTEEM

Before discussing the identifying elements, it is important to clarify the difference between general self-esteem and states of self-esteem. Most instruments used to measure self-worth, such as the Rosenberg Self-Esteem Scale, address broad elements that tend to be stable over time. These tools, while valuable, do not determine fluctuations that may be based on situational factors like work performance, academic success, social acceptance, or relationships. Kernis and his colleagues discovered that people with unstable self-esteem have more fluctuations based on circumstances, and have greater swings in self-perception (the differences in self-views from one day to the next are larger than for those with stable self-esteem). Kernis and others developed instruments aimed at measuring instability in situational self-worth. Deci and others created instruments designed to assess contingent self-worth. Many of these tools are not easily accessible by coaches and might require an industrial or organizational psychologist to assist with scoring and interpretation. Fortunately, management coaches can use observations and reviews of a client's experiences to detect trends in thinking styles and selected behaviors, then tailor coaching to support changes in self-talk and decision-making.

> *"...tailor coaching to support changes in self-talk and decision-making."*

Drawing from the work of Kernis, Deci, Ryan, and their associates, a composite list of characteristics emerges. These factors are presented in the following table.

Table 1: Composite List of Identifying Features in Individuals with Fragile High Self-Esteem

Characteristic	Examples
Motivated to shield positive feelings of self-worth—supports such positive feelings through self-promotion	Makes statements drawing attention to accomplishments and/or to connections with those in high positions, often when such information is unnecessary or off-topic; turns the conversations back to himself/herself to highlight his/her actions/skills; perceived as susceptible to flattery.

Criticizes those who are perceived as a threat to self-worth, and pushes away negative feedback as baseless	Uses emotional, personal language attempting to discredit someone who has provided negative feedback or someone who did not like the approach taken; often belligerent; will make comments like "he's just a coward" or "she's just jealous" or "that's so ridiculous I won't even address it"
Self-sabotages when concerned he/she will not succeed in reaching an important goal	Dresses too casually for a meeting with a senior leader regarding a project; begins expressing doubts and vocally focusing on problems as deadline approaches; fails to communicate delays
When threatened, may overstate skills and take large risks that can lead to self-inflicted job problems	When deadline missed, promises to double output by next milestone; procrastinates and then rushes when deadlines are looming; declares he/she will "go it alone" when the only way to meet project goals is through work with others; fails to report lost revenues or other problems, reasoning he/she can "pull it out" before the issues come to light

Highly protective and aggressive when self-worth is challenged; over time these reactions lead to problems in building trust and effective relationships	Develops reputation for being unable to take "bad news" well and attacking the messenger; employees avoid telling him/her about concerns or problems because of a lack of trust; peers consider the person "inconsistent" in his/her reactions (sometimes confident, sometimes outgoing, sometimes aggressively defensive). Examples: one time, an employee might share that he/she did not make a sales quota because of a personal illness, and the manager would be considerate and supportive; another employee might explain that her team didn't make quota because of the same individual who was sick, and that employee is berated and disciplined. There may be differences in reactions based on gender; sometimes women may be more likely to become passive-aggressive and depressive, withdrawing and becoming uncommunicative. Such behaviors will also lead to issues in employee trust and being able to form productive peer relationships.

"Such behaviors will also lead to issues in employee trust and being able to form productive peer relationships."

Significant swings in feelings from positive to negative self-worth and back again	Mood greatly affected by positive or negative work events, particularly if he/she perceives the event as supporting or reducing his/her perceived strengths; significant variations in view of self-worth from day to day. For example, the person might arrive in the morning in great spirits, but be despondent after a tough meeting in the afternoon, and then be in a better mood again when a compliment is paid to the person by a co-worker late in the day. There is a tendency to obsess about recent events, particularly if he/she is concerned they will reflect negatively on his/her reputation related to skills and knowledge. For example, if in the meeting that day, the person believed he/she was shown up for not knowing certain information, he/she will worry about the impact going forward, believing the incident will be long-remembered by others, even though in actuality the event was forgotten by the time the meeting had ended.

"Significant swings in feelings from positive to negative self-worth and back again."

Hyper-responsive to events (internal or external) that he/she believes are relevant to self-esteem—even when others may not view those events as related to the person's ego or sense of self-worth	Seen as emotionally reactive, often out of scale to the actual importance of the event (as viewed by others); may feel inadequate or upset simply by thinking another person is more skilled or more knowledgeable, even when no external issue has arisen to prompt such thinking. Others may be confused, trying to figure out what triggers certain responses. As an example, the manager could be very negative about hiring a certain individual that others think would be a good choice, because the manager feels threatened by the person's education, even though the manager has a master's degree in a different specialty area.

"Seen as emotionally reactive, often out of scale to the actual importance of the event... Others may be confused, trying to figure out what triggers certain responses."

When describing events, focuses on aspects that appear to be related to evaluation of self; interprets neutral or tangential information as important; associates a specific outcome in time with the long-term interpretation of self-worth	Others may interpret the focus as self-absorbed ("you think it's always about you") but for the individual, most interactions and events are viewed with the possibility of positive or negative impacts to self-esteem. May be described by others as "thin-skinned" in some situations. As work performance is often a major source of feedback, individuals with fragile high self-esteem are often intensely scanning the environment for recognition or possible threats to reputation (which feed or starve the continual need for external reinforcement of self-worth). For example, someone might make a passing negative comment in a meeting ("the manager didn't seem to be aware of the change") and that manager will interject explanations and pointed comments related to the statement during the rest of the meeting, even though everyone else has moved on to other topics.

"...focuses on aspects that appear to be related to evaluation of self..."

Seems to have more self-esteem events that he/she interprets negatively on a regular basis	Because of the increased focus on external events and situational conditions, the individual tends to over-interpret the meaning in things and is rocked by daily ups and downs—tense interactions or harsh comments have a greater impact. Others may be surprised by the growing pessimism they perceive with this manager, the regular way the person interprets actions as somehow "against" him/her.

More likely to become depressed	Based on the person's way of explaining things to himself/herself, the energy dedicated to environmental scanning, and the person's reactivity, the individual is more likely to fixate on mistakes and negative feedback in ways that limit productivity and functioning. Such factors have been shown to contribute to depression. In men, this may translate into anger and irritability, while in women this may translate into withdrawal and emotional resignation.

"...tends to over-interpret the meaning in things..."

Uses internal self-talk that overgeneralizes the results of one event to explain general life outcomes—every negative event becomes another example of "proof" of a life-long story of "failed" outcomes or missed opportunities because of some fatal personal flaw	Related to the work of Martin Seligman (explanatory styles related to pessimism/optimism); the manager tends to have excessively negative self-talk and thought distortions. Overgeneralization means the person will have one setback (or will have had a setback in the past) that colors all future decisions. Landmark negative events are referred to fairly frequently in conversations (e.g. passed over for promotion or aborted project or a personal experience such as divorce). The person may mention an event as though it took place recently; others will be surprised to discover the event occurred a number of years in the past.
Uses internal self-talk that overstates personal shortcomings as permanent yet may come across to others as unwilling to acknowledge personal flaws	Tends to believe his/her character limitations are to blame, rather than situational factors (e.g. being "stupid" rather than seeing a failure as due to timing or lack of resources). He/she is driven to mask the perceived character flaws and at the same time struggles with a desire to achieve and move forward. Others will overhear the manager being "hard" on himself/or herself after a problem arises, then a few minutes later, seeming to "crow" about his/her winning accomplishments and attributes.

Less resilient in stressful environments (not effective in coping skills); tense when pursuing personal goals	Takes longer to return to a normal mood after a setback linked to self-image; has difficulty remaining centered and becomes more "wound up" (worried rather than energized) when pursuing personal goals that he/she views as linked to self-image. May be seen as having an uneven track record—accomplishes great things in difficult conditions in the shorter term, but seems to withdraw or lose focus in the longer-term. People often tell this person "you're so tense!" or "you're trying too hard" or "you need to let things roll off your back more often."

Shifting sense of self; less-skilled in self-management and prone to self-doubt, which the person attempts to disguise with a tendency to take actions designed to create a specific image of a risk-taker and "major player"	In coaching conversations, individual moves between statements of confidence, drawing attention to achievements, and the recounting of decision-making processes that reveal insecurities— uncertainty in own skills, questioning the motives of others, looking to read "between the lines" in the statements of boss, peers, or subordinates. May make a statement revealing insecurity, followed by a plan of action that will overcompensate for the implied issue or character flaw (perceived in self or others).

"...attempts to disguise..."

Lack of specificity in self-definition	May come across as a conundrum of opposites—strong and confident in one way, and at the same time, uncertain of place in things and standings with other people. Can be overly confident in areas of accomplishment/ competency, yet unaware of other strengths and underestimating others' positive perceptions. May come across as a chameleon – seems to match different audiences, presenting somewhat different personas and priorities based on the people involved in ways that move beyond normal social adaptability.

Over-emphasis on the importance of skills, knowledge, and achievements in describing self-value	When meeting others, tends to recite résumé as though it defines who he/she is and this may come across in coaching. Stresses education or certifications or title or social standing, even when such information is not relevant in the conversation. Has difficulty describing self in terms that are not related to accomplishments, or describing activities that do not link to achievements in some way

"...a conundrum of opposites..."

Tendency to want to get back at others when sense of self is threatened and often has desire to vent about the perceived slights (more often men) or tendency to turn anger inward, feeling guilty and take feelings out on others who were not involved in the precipitating incident (more often women)	Will often voice frustrations /complaints to whoever is nearby, and repeat the story of the negative event a number of times without reaching any insights or making positive plans for action. The level of emotion will be intense, sometimes uncomfortable to others who may not understand the reason for the focus of energy. May discuss ways to retaliate; sometimes females may select passive-aggressive responses, such as delaying work or failing to pass along information. May be heard expressing displeasure with co-workers or subordinates when there are minor problems, vocalizing irritation that exceeds the value of the specific issue.

A few important aspects should be noted when reflecting on the information contained in the table. The management coach should listen for verbal cues and review session notes to observe trends over time. Historical patterns are significant. Further, the coach will want to reflect on clusters of characteristics—one or two elements would not likely indicate unstable self-esteem, and it would be rare for an individual to display all of the features mentioned. To gain a complete picture, it will be helpful to gather feedback from others—perceptions, recounting of critical incidents, or 360-degree instrument results if available.

"Historical patterns are significant."

COACHING TECHNIQUES FOR UNSTABLE HIGH SELF-ESTEEM

Given the nature of the person's internal dialogue and potential for defensiveness, it is not beneficial to discuss the concept of unstable or fragile high self-esteem directly. Using the executive's own examples and offering probing questions for reframing will support the client in developing conscious awareness of patterns and negative impacts. It is also essential to provide positive statements first that acknowledge the person's expertise and competencies, then delve into behavior that may be creating problems for that individual with a focus on defining what they want the behavior to be and the desired outcomes that result.

Clearly, it is important to create awareness of how the behaviors become barriers to the executive's work goals and to empower the individual in choosing how to shift behaviors. The coach cannot address formative experiences that shaped early self-esteem, nor is the coach responsible for repairing the person's sense of self-worth. Effective deployment of tools and meaningful questioning can lead to significant improvements from detracting behaviors.

As fragile high self-esteem individuals are often focused on success and achievements in work performance, they are often motivated to complete activities they recognize as contributing to improved work outcomes. In situations where management coaching has been suggested or required to help the person get back on track, it is possible to link the coaching exercises and dialogue to defined behavioral goals, such as building better trust with peers and subordinates, reducing feelings of stress and irritation at work, or finding ways to sustain positive energy and focus when receiving stressful feedback.

The executive coach observes triggers and works to frame discussions in terms of strengths and competencies the person

141

already possesses and values in relation to self-esteem. This approach helps avoid defensive responses and shutting down in the interactions. The coach also draws on effective performance examples from the client's past to help make connections between successful previous behaviors or decision-making and current opportunities.

Rapport and trust are established with the client over the first two or three sessions, allowing the individual to share his/her experiences and adequately consider trends and patterns. It is valuable to remember the unstable high self-esteem manager may come across as confident in these early sessions, striving to project competence in many areas. The coach may wish to strategically engage the individual with a few questions designed to investigate triggers and defense mechanisms. Simply asking, "when do you feel defensive?" could provide enlightening clues into self-talk and self-perceptions.

> *"The coach may wish to strategically engage the individual with a few questions designed to investigate triggers and defense mechanisms."*

If the management coach is being brought in to work with the individual for pre-determined reasons, the information provided before the initial coaching session helps the coach be aware of the relevance of self-esteem stability in a particular case. It is beneficial to listen for certain key words describing the individual such as: *aggressive, hostile, very defensive, intense, reactive, thin-skinned, volatile, moody, bragging, passive-aggressive, can be withdrawn, takes unnecessary risks, thinks highly of himself/herself, or personalizes everything.* These are often recommendations to explore the client's self-esteem profile in more detail.

Here are some question types that may be helpful during coaching sessions:

Reframing Questions
• What are some other motivations that might explain that person's actions?
• What are other ways of interpreting the events that took place?
• What would happen if you decided the 'story' regarding why certain things took place was no longer valid for you?
Self-Awareness Questions
• Describe what you were thinking and feeling when you said that/did that.
• What initiated that response?
• In reflecting on that situation, what are some thoughts and feelings the other person might have been experiencing?
• When have you taken this approach in the past? What were the outcomes? How were the outcomes the same or different now? What factors do you attribute the results to?

Goal Questions
• In what ways does that action plan match your leadership/personal goals?
• Describe how that action moved you towards or away from your goals in the situation.

One beneficial exercise involves the client practicing reframing through writing. The individual writes down his/her self-talk commentary related to a problem or negative event, then writes down new statements that incorporate other perspectives, facts, and non-judgmental or positive interpretations of the issues. The act of transcribing the thoughts helps the person develop objectivity and builds skills in understanding where perceptions and self-evaluations have become distorted. The client completes the activity as a homework assignment, then discusses the results with the coach in a follow-up session. This exercise can be repeated several times as new situations are encountered that seem to negatively impact the person's self-esteem. The person will learn about himself/herself and begin making changes in thought patterns when he/she is accountable for recognizing and evaluating unproductive beliefs and is also responsible for developing the alternatives.

Two other aspects are useful to consider when working with managers who have fragile high self-esteem: self-stories can be challenged and resiliency is a skill to cultivate. Because the person with unstable self-worth tends to create internal narratives that continually weave the past into the present the client often needs help in decoupling past experiences from current conditions. For example, having difficulties with a previous boss does not mean the client will have issues with a current boss— thoughts must be shifted to prevent self-fulfilling prophecies. To accomplish this decoupling, the coach guides the client to challenge assumptions about the previous experiences and stops the client when he/she starts to explain the story.

> *"...self-stories can be challenged and resiliency is a skill to cultivate."*

Similarly, people with fragile high self-esteem are often obsessed with whether and how things are likely to go wrong in the future. Again, it is important to bring the client back to a focus on the present. The coach stops the dialogue on negative projections of the future and re-directs the conversation to immediate next steps and guided imagery of success.

Managers with fragile high self-esteem tend to have limited coping skills. Their natural responses to stress often include:

- Irritability and belligerence (or withdrawal)
- Working harder (longer hours, more obsessive focus on details)
- Defensiveness
- Lack of care for physical health (skipping meals; not exercising; not getting enough sleep)
- Isolation and paranoia (distrustful of coworkers and/or direct reports; limited interactions with others outside of meetings)
- Increasing absenteeism (sick more often; late to work)

Significant progress can be made with these clients by emphasizing activities that build resiliency and addressing the importance of methods that relieve pressures. The coach serves to create awareness so the client recognizes signs of stress and triggers. The coach helps the client create an action plan that maintains mental balance and sustains the person's cognitive and interpersonal skills. The activities must be adaptable to work situations (in the office and during travel). The coach supports the client in incorporating these behaviors on a regular basis, creating new habits. The goal is to manage stress levels and develop consistency in moods, decision-making, and social behaviors with others.

Here is a brief list of suggested stress management activities that work with managers' busy schedules:

Stress Management Techniques
5-15 minute walk outside the building
15-30 minutes in a car listening to positive or calming music or taking a power-nap (person can move car to another parking lot if he/she is concerned about being seen by others)
5-10 minutes with stress-reducing smartphone application: e.g. nature sounds, simulation of fish tank, binaural sounds (right-brain/left brain balancing
5-10 minutes of journaling (kept on personal, non-company-owned electronic notebook or handwritten and shredded each day to ensure privacy)
30 minutes of daily exercise (walking, swimming, Pilates)
3 yoga sessions per week (yoga has been shown to improve mood and limit depression)
7 hours of sleep per night with ½ hour of quiet time (no television or computer use) before bed

These suggested questions and tools provide templates for focused coaching actions. Management coaches have other exercises and question sets that are equally effective; the target areas are provided to assist coaches in choosing strategies that best fit the client and his/her specific opportunities for growth.

MAKING PROGRESS

Each client provides unique strengths and challenges. Personality, external circumstances, and stress levels are all be factors contributing to observed behaviors. Consideration of the individual's state of self-esteem is another lens to understand the basis for stated issues in leadership of others and in self-control. This lens can help differentiate root causes and enable a coach to more rapidly pinpoint effective strategies for desired behavioral changes.

> *"Consideration of the individual's state of self-esteem is another lens to understand the basis for stated issues in leadership ..."*

In working with a middle manager who was an internal client, I was able to determine, through dialogue and observation, that this person had been identified as aggressive, defensive, overly confident, and a show-off by others. The individual was struggling with recent events the person viewed as failures at work, and building stress that was interfering with decision-making and their professional relationships with others. Over a period of six months, we used reframing and increased self-awareness, combined with stress management exercises to help the individual regain footing. Co-worker relationships and decision-making improved. The person continued as a successful manager within the organization, guided by a better understanding of self and improved coping skills. This executive also shifted in self-perceptions and learned to maintain a more balanced perspective of competencies and limitations while developing the ability to remain centered in times of intense pressure.

Kernis proposed that authenticity was a hallmark of stable self-esteem. He suggested individuals with optimal self-esteem accept themselves (strengths and flaws), do not shift energy and mood based on contingencies such as work performance or social standing, and do not engage in protective actions like defensiveness or emphasis on accomplishments when meeting others. Individuals with stable high self-esteem take others at face value. They exhibit well-being through self-acceptance, positive interactions in most social settings, consideration of actions through consistently applied internal standards, and a focus on personal growth. Management coaches help individuals with fragile high self-esteem develop a healthier self-concept, supporting their choices for behavioral changes that allow the person to transition to a new state of authentic self-confidence and positive self-perception. The client will achieve new levels of professional and personal success.

> *"Individuals with stable high self-esteem take others at face value."*

 Nicole Stragalas is the Executive Director of Stradivarius Solutions, a consulting firm specializing in organization development and training services. She also teaches as a Certified Advanced Facilitator for University of Phoenix.

Ms. Stragalas has served at the Director level in organizational development for several Fortune 100 companies and been published in several periodicals and books.

She is recognized for effective career coaching and management coaching approaches, and is a Certified Professional Coach as well as a Senior Professional in Human Resources and a Six Sigma Green Belt.

executivedirector@stradivarius-solutions.com
Stradivarius-solutions.com
888-588-9558

149

COACHING AND CHRISTIANS
Sharon Wilcox

In honor of all different beliefs, while this chapter provides valuable insights for everyone, I do want to let you know now that it is written with a focus on coaching Christians and coaching from a Christian perspective, so when reading it please be aware of this intention and simply adapt the concepts appropriately.

The belief that fate is pre-determined or controlled by a higher power may lead some to the conclusion that aspiring to goals is inappropriate. Others feel that to work with a coach means taking advice because they mistakenly believe the mentor role is that of the coach. Some feel that the direction for all they do comes through prayer and that independent thinking or exploration is different than using prayer for guidance. For a Christian, a barrier to engaging a coach is that they want their focus to be on God and their direction to be from God. Based on the teachings of the bible, coaching does make sense and fits with God's plan. This chapter explores that perspective.

EVERYONE HAS A JOURNEY

I have memorized a lot of verses over the years; I have claimed Jeremiah 29:11 as my own. I hold tightly on this promise which is one of hundreds that God has given me. I know that different from man, God keeps all promises. If you are not familiar with Jeremiah 29:11 you are probably wondering why it pertains to coaching? Well, God says he knows the plans he has for you, plans to not harm you, plans to prosper you, to give you hope, and a future.

If that is so, then why would a Christian need a coach? If God is in control of your life then it seems like all the answers are

151

available. What to do, when to do it, and how to go about it. Each question begs an answer that should be easily available. The answers are available in his word and through reading his word, the Bible, one becomes more knowledgeable. At the same time, the Bible does state that everyone should seek wise counsel. Proverbs 15:22: Plans fail for lack of counsel but with many advisers they succeed. I consider wise counsel a resource. This resource comes in many different forms: parent, sibling, documentary, book, article, friend, coach, attorney, movie, blog, teacher, internet article, attending a class or conference, business owner, or even a stranger. You are probably thinking that you would never take advice from a stranger; you probably have many more times than you remember. Did you personally know the critic who wrote the restaurant blog and persuaded you to try the new restaurant that opened recently?

I recently gave advice to a couple that was debating where to hang out on a Friday night. A friend and I were leaving a restaurant after a scrumptious meal of coconut shrimp and listening to a trio of musicians on the upper deck that were stomping out some oldies we both could sing too. I wanted to dance, but held myself back in fear I would be trampled by the 40-year-olds that were all celebrating their birthdays. As we descended the stairs, we encountered the couple on the outside sidewalk having a discussion on where to go next. I did not know them and they did not know me; normally I would not have interrupted anyone's conversation. I was feeling hospitable, friendly, and confident. Since they were standing directly in my path, I stopped. Clearly I could sense the woman was interested in checking out Coconut Joe's as she was commenting on the music to the male companion and he was hesitant. Anyway, I added my opinion, unsolicited, about what a fun time it would be to go to the upper deck and that there was no cover charge. Plus the food was delicious so if they decided to eat dinner, they were in for a treat. They thanked me, or maybe she thanked me after he said okay, and they proceeded to head towards the stairs to check it out. Hopefully that was a successful night for both. They had a decision to make and chose to listen to counsel, someone outside their realm of expertise, and made the choice to check out the upper deck.

Now giving advice differs from being a coach. A coach is there to help you figure out what is already inside of you. A coach will allow you to explore many possibilities without judgment or bias. A coach does not necessarily need to be an expert in the field you are exploring.

> *"A coach is there to help you figure out what is already inside of you."*

Sometimes an objective person will allow you to explore your ideas more fully. The coach will ask questions for clarification that gives you an opportunity to communicate a dream, hope, or goal that may have been tucked away in your memory for another day. In Psalm 20:4, David says "may the Lord give you the desires of your heart and make all of your plans succeed." You will decide if and when you will write a plan on paper for obtaining your heart's desires. Be aware of your motives in any plans that you make. We are warned that making plans without the right motive and without our Lord being in the center is not what we should be doing. 2 Corinthians 1:17 and Isaiah 29:15 both speak to this.

We all have a choice on how we go about that process. Sometimes we seek someone that can guide us on how to go about it and that is when a coach would be most helpful. A coach is objective and impartial about what choices you make. The coach is there to help you with YOUR Journey in life. If a coach is giving you advice or persuading you to make other choices that are more to their morals, values, or missed opportunities then they are not really a coach. As individuals, Christian or not, we already have an inkling of the plan inside of us; to put it in action may take additional exploration and planning. If we will commit to the Lord whatever we do, he will establish those plans according to Proverbs 16:3. Even so, Proverbs 16:9 states that in our hearts we humans plan our course; the Lord establishes our steps. A coach can help you with the plan to determine what steps to take.

> **"A coach is objective and impartial about what choices you make."**

Getting back to my question of why does a Christian need a coach? Several things come to mind: we have desires and God knows the desires of our hearts. He does want to keep his promise of providing every good gift and the desires of our heart if it is good and if it aligns with his plans to further his purpose. It makes sense to explore every desire to determine if it is truly from God or just a worldly desire that is not meant to further his purpose. Ways you explore include seeking wise counsel, presenting your ideas, seeking perspective, hear your ideas rephrased back to you, and having someone probe and clarify. Proverbs 19:20 states we should listen to advice and accept discipline, and at the end you will be counted among the wise. Of course, the first and foremost is to pray that God reveals the truth to you and that he will make the way for it to happen. Our heavenly Father is who we should go to first. By spending time in our prayer closet and praying, listening and talking with him about what we think our ideas are and what he thinks of those desires, we open ourselves to guidance. Proverbs 19:21: "Many are the plans in a person's heart; it is the Lord's purposes that

154

prevail." If it is not his will for you then all the pieces will not come together easily or you may move ahead too quickly or slowly and the outcome will be different than expected. The Lord cautions us that if we continue to carry out plans that are not his we will heap sin upon sin Isaiah 30:1. Reevaluation of plans, goals, and desires is appropriate and helps to determine if you are still on the right path. A coach might ask you to put your plan in writing to refer back to so you can visualize what it is you are working towards; you may meet with them on a regular schedule to ensure progress and accountability. They may also ask you to use affirmation statements so that you visualize yourself being successful in your journey wherever it may take you - this supports your success.

> *"Reevaluation of plans, goals, and desires is appropriate and helps to determine if you are still on the right path."*

ARE WE THERE YET?

Sometimes long-range plans need to be changed due to various reasons. It could be financial backing is not available, obstacles were presented that could not be handled at the same time, or maybe even that the desires became more defined. "Sometimes the Lord may put obstacles in the way," Jeremiah 6:21 "because he has something better planned," Hebrews 11:40. Working with a coach you may want to revisit the goals that were defined earlier to determine if they still fit the desire. As God leads us in a direction that we thought was where we were meant to go, he may reveal to you through prayer and even another individual that the direction has changed. The change could be monumental or slightly tweaked because of what he is wanting to accomplish. God himself is the master planner from the beginning with the creation of the world in 6 days to Jesus's betrayal and being nailed to the cross. Even Jesus, his only begotten Son, could not change his journey. He followed it perfectly. He asked that it be taken away; to please his Father he knew that it was his destiny that God's will be done and it was as God himself planned. As a Christian, it is often times we forget that God is in control and we think we have all the answers until he reminds us and he shows us that we do not. Ideally we are seeking his answers earnestly by reading, studying, and searching his word for his will for our lives. It is his desires to accomplish his purpose that we are well-served to remember. Once this is revealed, then our plans may change. If the plans are meant to change and don't change, things may turn out poorly because his purpose was thwarted Job 5:12. He thwarts the plans of the crafty, so that their hands achieve no success. With a coach you explore where you are at the moment, how things transpired, and what you intend to do about it. Perhaps the timing is not right and you are intended to wait on some other things to develop before you move forward. God has a way of using other people to direct this and to put other people in our paths that may benefit us. Sometimes through our lives, God may use our life to affect others. The life lesson may not be meant for us, it may be meant for someone else.

Our journey through life can be remarkable or not, this depends on our outlook of life. One often hears the question, "Is the glass half empty or half full?" What is your perspective? Often success is measured against the wrong things. Some examples of success measures are: how much money you make, what size of home you live in, where you live, what type of car you drive, brand name clothes you wear, expensive jewelry, job titles, business you work for, or even where you vacation each year. You choose: Is this what life truly is about? Remember, these things are temporary. Once you die and when your obituary is read, what will others remember about you? Are these things listed? I can't remember the last time I saw any of these material things listed. Most obituaries list family members, organizations you were a member of, and any contributions you made as an individual to make life better. What is your legacy? What lasting impression do you want to make on society? Material things or worldly things are not of God, they are of man. You have a choice to live for God or to live focused on what you have and status. Depending on whether you have made a choice and what it is, you have defined your journey. Is it what you want or do you want to change it? Each day is a gift and the gift can be unopened and kept only by you or you can choose to open it, cherish it, and share with others. These decisions can be explored and supported with the help of a coach. A coach will help you figure out your life. How do you want to live? What is the big picture when small things continue to clog up daily life? Coaching will help you think beyond today and plan for tomorrow. Coaching will help you determine what is important to you and only you.

> *"Coaching will help you determine what is important to you and only you."*

Perhaps you are familiar with the story of Moses taking the Israelites through the desert to the Promised Land. God promised them a better life, yet they had doubts and didn't have a vision of where they were going. They travelled for 40 years in the wilderness before arriving. They could have gotten there sooner had they had faith in God to bring them through. Instead they tried to do it on their own and lost sight. They complained about the food and what they were eating and often wanted to go back into slavery so that they could eat better. Really??? Moses coached them; they had to make their own choice of whether or not to reevaluate the plan of action. Moses didn't know what was best for each one, only they knew and the Lord. At one point the Israelites were complaining about being in the desert and dying there. Moses was interceding on their behalf and the Lord was getting tired of their complaining so he told Moses to tell them to move on. This is what a coach does. They can be a cheerleader, motivator, and encourager as well as providing a process so you expand your vision. Were the Israelites affirming their decision to be freed from captivity? Probably not! They did not understand that freedom from slavery was better because they thought that eating better was more important. They were short sighted and had not looked beyond their current situation. This biblical story is an example of life not being done alone. It shows that you do include other people; sometimes they are there to help and you could be thinking the help was just for you – truly it was for both of you. Yes, sometimes the Journey is going to be tough and you are going to want to give up and quit. Life Coaches are there to help you through that time by knowing when to discuss a new topic or just inquire about what is going on right now. What is giving you concern and how can they help you through that? Perseverance to continue is also one of the fruits of the spirit in Galatians 5:17. When you feel like giving up, that is just God asking to have his job back.

Sometimes we take over what he is better at doing and try to do it ourselves. We begin to worry and become frustrated and feel like the whole world is on our shoulders because nothing seems to go right. This is the time to pray, pray diligently and unceasingly. Ask forgiveness for trying to do God's job because we do it so poorly and are meant to handle only things we as humans have control over. We also want to remember to ask God for his continued blessings as he continues to keep his promises. James

5:11 speaks to this - it says those who have persevered are counted as blessed. The Lord brought about good for Job after his perseverance. The Lord is full of compassion and mercy. More importantly when you persevere doing the will of God, you will receive what he has promised Hebrews 10:36. Remember Jeremiah 29:11? Even when we think we have been forgotten, this promise is ours. If through prayer you do not get the peace you were seeking, then maybe you were on the wrong path.

FINDING PEACE AND JOY IN OBEDIENCE

When you are doing God's will and you are serving him according to his purpose, then you will have peace. You will be filled with joy as you live out the purpose that has been defined and that you have finally started to follow. Peace and joy go hand in hand; I don't think you can have one without the other. Now, to get to the point of having peace, you may want a coach to ask you the questions that will define the journey that you are meant to be on. When the questions are asked, then you can verbalize the answers that you have known that were buried and unspoken before. Have the decisions you made brought you joy? Do you have peace about the decisions you have made? Are they intertwined or not? How important is joy to you? How important is Peace to you? What will it take to get there? What obstacles do you perceive? What if you can't obtain Joy? What if you can't obtain Peace? Where will you go from here? Delving into oneself and being introspective is an opportunity to truly get to the heart of what is important. This is a crucial step to finding joy and peace.

> *"...you may want a coach to ask you the questions that will define the journey..."*

Being obedient in your journey may require sacrifice. As a child did you want to please your Mother or Father? The reason you wanted to please your Mother or Father was because you loved them. You also thought as a child that if you didn't do something your parents may not love you. As an obedient child of our heavenly Father it is love that propels you to walk in obedience to his commands. From the very beginning his first command is to love him. Then why would you not want to please your heavenly Father by being obedient to him? The Father requires obedience above all. Psalm 128:1 states that we are blessed when we fear the Lord, when we walk in obedience to him. We also show him our love. Every action good or bad reflects whether or not we were obedient. Each one has consequences. I am more inclined to want good consequences instead of bad don't you?

Being a Christ follower is unique. There are diverse religions today and that is different from being a Christ follower. Following Christ is sometimes not understood by other people. Even other Christians may question the decisions and choices you make. You will uniquely follow the voice that Jesus speaks to you. It may seem crazy by others, or not practical. Remember, sometimes the sacrifice is required to carry out God's purpose and will for your life. Even if you believe you know where you should be going on the journey, you will eventually question that. Having a coach to assist you through these times will be helpful in defining the purpose and your understanding of the journey. Interesting enough as you journey through life, in addition to experiencing blessing in your life, others around you will also be blessed. Sometimes that is how it works; the purpose may be to bring others to Christ or to provide a blessing. Obedience is better than sacrifice (1 Samuel 15:22b). It may be a challenge or sacrifice for someone to seek wise counsel; the benefits will bring peace and joy. It is said that people are placed in our path for a season or lifetime. Ecclesiastes 3:1, "There is a time for everything, and a season for every activity under heaven." Every season may bring something new, it depends on your calling. Your calling can change depending on what God wants to have done. It is often very challenging and of course our God doesn't always promise the easy path. What he did promise was eternal life (1 John 2:5). Even though we talk about our desires, dreams, and goals (or however you want to refer to our future) with a coach and map out a plan, it may become clear that it there is a time to go a different way. I guess that is why re-evaluations of the path are done periodically. Sometimes in life we get thrown a curve ball and the catch changes the next step. A coach can help you during that defining moment to make sense of it all.

Several years ago I had my first experience with coaching. I was able to be coached by several individuals. At that time, I knew that I wanted to make changes in my life though I was not sure at the time what changes those entailed. After a very intense 4-day session, I came away with a renewed sense of purpose and goals. I was able to determine a plan and have been working it ever since. It has been a slow process; it is worth every effort that I have given. I knew that I wanted to be obedient to God in whatever way he intended. I am very close to financial independence. I am leading a small group of women that I minister to on a weekly basis as I pray and study the word. I have a church home and attend regularly. I am also part of a small singles group that studies the bible and shares life together under the direction of a group leader that has a passion to love and seek God's word for guidance in this world where we live. I have also met a wonderful man that shares my faith and my heart to serve God. I am still waiting and seeking earnestly what it is that God wants me to do for the next part of my journey.

> *"A coach can help you during that defining moment to make sense of it all."*

Sharon Wilcox is a native of Charleston, South Carolina. Grew up in the Catholic faith and attended a private school in the early years. She always thought she would grow up to be a Nun; however, had no idea what this entailed or the sacrifice that would be involved. Her family moved and the decision was made to attend public school. Life changed while in her early 20's when she became a Christian. It wasn't until January 2005 that her relationship with Christ began to deepen. Since that time she has led small groups of women in bible studies, coached and sought God's will for her life.

She completed her undergraduate studies at Charleston Southern and graduated with Honor's upon receiving her MS in Computer Resources from Webster University. She has over 28 years in a Human Resources career and became a Certified Mediator in 2009. Traveled to Florida to attend a coaching class and has coached for over two years now. Resides in a small town where everybody knows everybody with her beautiful daughter, Sarah and adventuresome son, Alex and yappy miniature dachshund, Minnie. She enjoys sports with her children, kayaking, biking, girlfriends, gardening, arts, travelling, music, reading and cooking while she waits for God's promises to be fulfilled.

shwilcox_1@homesc.com

162

Defining Your Journey to Success: Career Coaching

Ahfeeyah Thomas

What does defining your journey to success truly mean? What does embarking on this journey require? In this chapter we will answer these questions; we will outline the steps to define and embark on your journey.

Each of us as individuals are given the opportunity to excel and to define our own path in life. Planning is a choice and gives us direction. Life changes may alter our plans; plans are fluid so anticipate flexing to changes.

Begin with the basics. To make any change or to start anything new, start with mentally understanding and breaking down the process. Let's begin with the words 'define' and 'journey' and 'success'.

- What does it mean to define? To define something means to give it meaning, to outline its purpose and potential.
- What does the word journey mean? What does it mean to go on a journey? Now for some of us this stretches our thinking because we perceive that journeys are long and require a lot of packing and provision. Merriam Webster defines a journey as any transition or travel from one place to another. The place might be physical or it might be in terms of thought - often times the word journey is used metaphorically. For example phrases like, "the journey from childhood to adolescence" or "the journey through time". Journey is used in the same context when we speak about our career path and our success. There is a goal and place that we hope to transition to, and the process to get there is our journey.

164

- What is success? As a career coach I believe everyone's definition is truly different and unique. According to the Merriam Webster Dictionary, success is a favorable or desired outcome; also the attainment of wealth, favor and eminence.

By "Defining My Journey to Success" I am giving meaning by outlining the potential and purpose of my transition from where I am to a favorable place where I achieve my desired outcome.

This is my company's tagline, Defining Your Journey to Success. I believe that this point of defining your personal success must be reached with every client that chooses to utilize the career coaching experience. This statement and definition provides an understanding that there are goals to be achieved. More than anything, at the end of this journey, the individual will be in a favorable and desired place. Career coaching supports defining and achieving goals. As a career coach, I work with a number of clients from all different backgrounds and with a variety of characteristics. One thing that is consistent, even with the many differences, is that these clients have a common end goal and that ultimately is the goal to succeed. Some clients want instant results; it is my obligation and commitment to the client to provide them a process for moving toward success. Coaching means doing this by asking the right questions, helping the client identify their skills and passions as it relates to their career path. A coach creates awareness that attaining success, the wealth, favor, and eminence, requires being equipped and ready.

> *"Career coaching supports defining and achieving goals."*

Preparation is one of the first challenges in the coaching experience because of the client's desire to obtain instant results. As a career coach, you have the knowledge and tools to provide a temporary fix; ethically you must ask, "Am I providing this client with a quality process and service? Am I empowering them to understand the journey and discover their steps towards achieving success?" Customer service starts with the premise that the customer is right. In coaching, a client is part of a strategic partnership; this is different than having a customer. While it is understood that there will be monetary compensation, a client is a person and in addition to the coach providing a service, the coach is creating a continued open door of communication and trust. A client may still be discovering the answers about how they wish to go about achieving their goals. As a coach, we must realize that our client has come to us for help and guidance. Our role, instead of making the decisions for the client, is to provide them with perspective and outlook. Ask your client to repeat the following question, and then respond aloud: "What does it mean to define my journey to success?"

> *"...the coach is creating a continued open door of communication and trust."*

Defining one's Journey to Success means preparation. It means being prepared for what one is setting out to accomplish, and being prepared for any opportunities or obstacles that arise along the way. In addition to the obstacles that our client may face, there are also opportunities. These opportunities are often overlooked because of a lack of preparation, so in defining the journey to success a coach partners with the client to expand thinking and challenge perceptions. Evaluate the pros and cons of opportunities and consider what it will take to be prepared. As a career coach, exploring some of the pros with our clients in their journey starts with this question: "What will this opportunity help you achieve?" After the client answers the question, the coach guides the client to go even deeper and asks the same question in regards to their 1 year, 2 year, 3 year, 5 year, and 10 year goals or plan. The client then has the opportunity to explore the idea and consider whether the path they are on is the right path for them. Again, create awareness around preparing. The power of asking the right questions is vital in the coaching experience. Ultimately as the coach we must understand the client and also expand the client's understanding of them self.

After exploring what the client wants, the coach asks the client about their barriers to achieving what they want in their career. Identifying the barriers creates the opportunity to next consider solutions for moving past the barriers.

Another area of preparation is asking the client what skills, tools, and other resources they have to achieve what they want. In addition to this supporting preparation for their journey to success, this also provides useful information for a resume.

It is amazing how often people forget that work in one kind of job often equates to skills that transfer to a totally different kind of job. Also for many people there are skills learned at home, volunteering, and in the community. Resources include different people, places to find out about jobs, and programs that help people in their careers. Developing a resume, networking, and formulating a job search strategy are preparation for discovering and then pursuing opportunities.

> ## "The power of asking the right questions is vital in the coaching experience."

AN EXAMPLE FROM PERSONAL EXPERIENCE

I have seen generations of people mistake what they know with what they love. My mother was one of three girls and she chose a different career path while her sisters chose the same career path as their mother, my grandmother. Growing up when I looked at this in my family, I thought nothing of it until I began to see the same trend in families of friends and others. I asked myself if this could be a coincidence, that these children of parents and grandparents that grew up in different times and under different circumstances and all loved the same craft. Because I lacked the understanding of how to ask questions then, I took some time later to think back on my family. My aunts worked between the hours of 11 PM and 7 AM while I was still very young. I would run to the stairs when I heard them approaching with laughter in front of the house every morning. I had always seen this as a sign of happiness. I look back now and remember the reason I ran to the stairs every morning, and that was to hear what had happened the night before. They talked about all of their co-workers who weren't doing their work and how it made them feel. I am proud of them today because each conversation began and ended in laughter and a determination to find a way around the obstacles they encountered the night before. I did often wonder why they stayed in their jobs given these conditions. Was it because this is what they knew and what worked for the matriarch of the family? Did they want to follow the example of the person they loved the most, or was this what they really enjoyed? I have never coached either of my aunts; I have heard the stressful stories and saw the

168

effects it had on the family. If I venture a guess, this is not what they loved to do. Were these two women successful in their journey? This is a question I cannot answer; I will say they did not move to a favorable place. One of my aunts now suffers with a brain tumor and struggles to make ends meet with the addition of her medical bills. My other aunt gave me a real wakeup call on life as we could have lost her after she suffered an aneurism at work and was not found for hours.

While I was neither around when their careers began nor a career coach while they encountered some of these issues, I can identify some of the benefits a career coaching process would have offered my aunts. One of my aunts is very organized, very detailed, positive, and extremely strong; most of all she is creative. Each challenge she faces she overcomes and in her determination she shows her smile. Could she have been an executive or a CEO? I would bet my life savings on her in this role and realize that she would love it! I believe strongly she could do it and would be happy doing it. She shines most when helping others while also maintaining order and organization at the same time. The position that she worked in did not allow her the opportunity to utilize any of these talents, skills, or passions.

In defining what the journey to success entails and in the pursuit of success, one step is to identify skills, talents, and passions. As a career coach, this is the beginning for creating success in any role. When my clients identify their skills, it helps them to identify themselves. It is a starting point for preparation, provides essential information for a resume, and then in an interview, what they have to offer and what they bring to the table comes out naturally.

What would a career coach have had to offer in the situation with my aunts? I believe this question directly impacted my decision to be a career coach, and also gave me the drive to commit to my profession. A career coach would have asked my aunts the questions that would cause them to think further than their comfort zone, to think further than what each knows as an individual. Also, a career coach would have provided perspective as well as resources to aid in the steps toward their success. For example, my one aunt may have considered and then become an executive or director if she desired – she could have had a vocation instead of just a job. My other aunt is not as detailed and doesn't enjoy being in charge or delegating tasks as much as her sister; she is very kind and warm, and passionate about cooking, children, and sewing. She speaks with a soft and warm tone, and is much more patient than both her sisters. Again, a career coach may have been beneficial in providing perspective by asking the right questions, and most of all helping her to identify her strengths and how to maximize her potential. She may have discovered an interest in teaching, nursing, social work, counseling, or something that again would have been a vocation. I am a devoted career coach today because of these women. From my mother I learned to be ambitious and pursue my dreams. She always knew she wanted to be an educator, and still finds joy as she shares her story of how she used to teach her dolls and stuffed animals as a child. Her passion grew as she pursued her education and goals. From my aunts I did learn that there will be obstacles and to just keep working hard. They may not have been in the ideal position; they committed to being the best at what they did. Now I seek both to be in a position that taps into what I love and also allows me to love serving and to love the people for whom I provide service.

I trust that you can see where commitment as a coach can be life changing for others. As we continue, consider that as a coach, helping the client define their journey to success sometimes includes us defining ours too. The skills and qualities we encourage our clients to identify then develop we must also identify and then develop.

> *"...as a coach, helping the client define their journey to success sometimes includes us defining ours too."*

TOOLS FOR THE JOURNEY TO A SUCCESSFUL CAREER

Our attitudes determine how we take on challenges and affect how we view things. I mentioned my aunt's and their determination. They came home and spoke of the ups and downs of their jobs, and they dedicated themselves to having a positive attitude and strong work ethic on the job. In defining our journey to success we must have a positive attitude. The ability to see things going in an unsatisfactory direction and still say "I can do this" is much different than feeling sorry and discouraged. In the midst of adversity we must find positivity. As coaches we are committed in the coaching process to model for our client how to speak and think positively. Coaching involves skill development, and positivity is a skill for clients to develop.

A coaching tool that I came across as I went through my coaching certification to develop the skill of positivity is an affirmation statement. In one's affirmation statement, the first step is identifying goals in all areas that the client wants to achieve, and then creating them into a one statement in present tense. One of the requirements when writing the affirmation statement is that the words are all positive. At this stage we are transitioning from defining the journey to success to implementing the skills to continue success. There is no such thing as 'trying' in success;

there is attitude and action. A thought is the gateway to dreams accomplished.

On a journey to success in a career, there are additional tools that support results. Coaching empowers clients with perspective for creating and implementing tools so clients are learning. When providing career coaching, there are times when it makes sense to offer coaching services in combination with training or consulting whether the coach also does the training and consulting or whether that is through a different service. The key is to clearly define the roles and if providing more than one type of service then identifying which role is used each step of the way.

"Coaching empowers clients..."

Whether through training, consulting, or coaching, because the process of finding and being offered a job is now very different each component of the process is explored in depth.

For example, resume writing has changed. Previously there was a one size fits all approach to resumes and now each resume is tailored specifically to a prospective employer. Before a resume was largely a job description and now it is important to quantify specific accomplishments instead. When a client knows how to write a great resume, then the role of a career coach is to look at it from the perspective of a potential employer and ask questions. The client may then discover things they want to change. If the client has a good resume, then a consultant makes some specific recommendations to enhance it. If a client is unsure about how to write a resume, then some training on resume styles and expectations makes sense.

Instead of searching the want ads for a job, social media sites and job boards are the places to find jobs and to get found. Enhancing opportunities may include cleaning up or creating profiles on LinkedIn, Twitter, and Facebook. If a client is savvy using the social media sites, then a coach looks at their profiles with them and asks questions. Alternatively a consultant may point out a few key areas to rework along with specific suggestions. If a client is unfamiliar with social media profiles, then training is important because the first place recruiters go is LinkedIn, many recruiters post using Twitter, and Facebook is used to check out job candidates.

Historically finding a job was about who you know; now more than ever employers want to know how fast a new employee can get up to speed. At the same time, it starts with a foot in the door. Networking does count and often companies prefer internal referrals for positions. A career coach asks a client about who they know and what their opportunities are for making people aware of their career search. Other options for networking include LinkedIn, job fairs, and of course professional membership events for organizations in the client's career field.

A comprehensive job search strategy includes preparing several types of resumes that are then tweaked for each potential employer, ensuring a strong online presence, actively networking both online and face-to-face, and continuing to build applicable skills. A career coach asks questions and expands thinking about possibilities for each of the components of a job search strategy. A consultant advises clients about additional steps. A trainer teaches about the various strategies and how to get started.

Bottom line, if a client knows about tools, resources, and strategies then the role of the career coach works well asking questions and bringing in different perspectives in preparation for how potential employers view everything. Alternatively for some clients, serving as a consultant provides them with a recommendation. If a client has limited knowledge, then training them may make sense. Talking with the clients about the different approaches means they choose which services they want and how to best move forward on their journey.

In the example I shared with my aunts, chances are what they really wanted for a career was simply buried because that was outside of the process they knew for finding a job. Their barriers included education, societal expectations, and immediate needs for income. With a coach, talking about how to move past these barriers means awareness and leads to action. My aunts may have found training opportunities, considered different kinds of jobs, and planned how to balance time looking for a job with their work schedules. Talking about job options might have sparked new ideas and motivation for my aunts. Chances are my aunts had many skills that they could have used in a resume and for a different career.

The next step I take with clients is practicing for interviews. Based on their career goals and strategy, the skills that they bring to the role they are seeking, and what a potential employer wants, it is essential clients know how to present themselves. I work with the client on what is called an elevator pitch and on interviewing.

An elevator pitch is a short summary used to sell a product, business idea, or even an organization; it lasts up to 60 seconds or the equivalent of the time for an elevator ride. Elevator pitches are traditionally used when networking. Clients may question the value of having an elevator pitch when they are not selling a product or business idea. The individual is the business idea and is the product. An opportunity may present itself at any time, and it is imperative to be prepared. After a good elevator pitch, the potential employer walks away having an understanding of who the individual is and how they can be of benefit to that employer. The elevator pitch also provides an opening for an interview. On a deeper level than that, the candidate that is prepared with a great elevator pitch is prepared for more effectively presenting them self on paper, online, and in person.

Interview preparation includes practicing different types of questions, discussing appearance, planning arrival time, considering what to have in your hands during an interview, and confidence.

Imagine a coach working with my aunts to practice interviewing for different jobs. In addition to be aware of new possibilities and being prepared for the interview process, my aunts would have built their confidence to make their journey to success real.

With so many potential job candidates and increased ways of recruiting, it is the job of the career coach to create the awareness of the client around how beneficial it is to stand out and be remembered. In today's world, employers are seeking out a variety of different avenues for screening clients, and are showing an interest in personal character.

In a world where LinkedIn, Twitter, and Facebook are used in the recruiting and hiring process, there is a whole new dynamic around preparation, the job search process, and the value of a career that is doing work you enjoy.

Career coaching has a very special meaning because it is carrying forward the legacy of my aunts and creating new possibilities for others to define their journey to success.

> *"...it is the job of the career coach to create the awareness of the client around how beneficial it is to stand out and be remembered."*

Ahfeeyah is a Certified Professional Coach and CEO at Trifecta Career Advisory, Inc. She offers services as a Career Coach, Professional Resume Writer, Image Consultant, Motivational Speaker and Staffing Specialist. She studied Business Management at Northeastern University and has also completed Human Resources Management certification. Ahfeeyah combines her knowledge in Business, Human Resources, and Coaching to educate her clients on topics such as Personal Branding and Staffing from the recruiter's eye.

Ahfeeyah has collaborated with Harvard Medical School K-12 Diversity Programs, Boston University Medical Center, and various other organizations and continues to educate in the New England area, giving hope to everyone that desires more than a position in life and seeks to define their journey to success. She believes that success is not an option - it is a must. She thanks you in advance for your time and the opportunity to be part of your journey to success.

Remember each journey began with a step. Take your step towards greatness today and contact me for more information.

www.trifectacareeradvisory.com
Athomas.Baptista@trifectacareers.com

BUILDING LEADERS AT
SIGMA-ALDRICH CORPORATION: A CASE STUDY
Erick Koshner

Most successful companies are striving to improve their talent and are investing in the next generation of leaders. Among the critical issues being addressed are:

- Who will lead the company in ten years?
- Are the right capabilities in place to achieve the business strategy?
- How are strategies to evolve in the coming years?
- How do leaders develop a culture of high performance that elevates success?

The effort becomes even more challenging both as attrition occurs due to retirements and as globalization/geographic expansion requires new, expanded capabilities. Given the importance of talent to strategy execution, global companies increasingly must enhance the strength of their leadership pipeline to meet future business needs. Consequently, succession planning and leadership development are critical elements of any large organization's strategic planning process.

> *"Most successful companies are striving to improve their talent and are investing in the next generation of leaders."*

In leadership development, it is important to make the distinction between how one is performing and how one is developing. Clearly, performance is critical. It focuses on getting the work done and is reflected in the results achieved. At the same time, if one focuses solely on performance, over the long-term they miss opportunities to significantly improve results in their current role or in a role to which they aspire.

Development, on the other hand, is reflected in improved knowledge, skills, behaviors, or new ways to thinking and approaching issues. Development requires defining clear objectives and putting a plan in place to reach the objectives. When framing development objectives and plans, it is important to have a framework and a development coach to serve as a guide to the process. Consequently, Sigma-Aldrich's executive development process begins with self-reflection, concentrating on three key areas:

- Where Am I Today?
  - Current and Previous Two Assignments
  - Major Experiences Gained
  - Acquired Skills/Competencies
- Where Do I Want To Go?
  - Long-Term Career Objectives (3-5 years)
  - Short-Term Career Objectives (1-2 years)
- How Will I Get There?
  - Experience/Skills Requirements
  - Plan to close the experience or skill gaps (development objectives)

A key to getting started with development is avoiding the trap of paralysis by analysis. Often there are conflicting views regarding whether to base one's development on existing strengths or on areas for improvement. The optimal path is a balanced approach. In recent years, a number of leadership experts have debated that development plans oftentimes focus too much on perceived weaknesses with the naïve expectation that leaders can maximize each and every competency and become perfectly well-rounded. The explanation is that if the leader has little talent in a given area, all the training programs and the best laid plans will fail to turn this gap into an asset. Alternatively, training for the weaknesses maximizes the potential, however limited, for improving those specific skills.

> ## *"The optimal path is a balanced approach."*

That being the case, the cornerstone of the approach employed within Sigma-Aldrich is to focus on one or two areas, preferably leveraging existing strengths and closing gaps or acquiring new skills which could limit further career growth if not in place. Areas selected could be:

- Functional/technical skills - knowledge, special capabilities, and competencies required for a given role or functional area, such as applied chemistry or finance
- Management skills - focusing on the business or associated processes such as strategic planning or marketing
- Leadership - focusing on the ability to lead and get results through others

SIGMA-ALDRICH LEADERSHIP: A YEAR IN THE LIFE OF LEADER DEVELOPMENT

The example below views leadership development from the important perspective of the client in a journal.

February

I just met with my manager to discuss my performance review from the previous year. Although development was not discussed directly, my boss reinforced many of my own thoughts on key strengths and my biggest opportunities for improvement. After the meeting, I began to think that other than attending one leadership course offered internally, I had not put much time or thought into my development over the past year. I will benefit from a better plan going forward. Although the training was solid, I have been assigned some pretty aggressive targets and will be expected to accomplish things more quickly and effectively than ever before.

March

A recent realignment of reporting relationships means I have a new boss and several new team members reporting to me. Not only do I need to modify several performance objectives, it is also time to begin working on my development plan. After completing my competency self-assessment, I met with my new boss to get his thoughts with regards to what areas of development I should be targeting for the year. After our discussion, I completed my development objectives in the on-line system, noticing several development suggestions are available for each competency. These seem to apply, so I incorporated several of them into my development plan. I am very busy, so happy to get this done and off my list of things to do.

April

It's already the second quarter and I have not thought about or done anything regarding my development since creating the plan in March. My new boss suggested I meet with someone from Organizational Development to review my development plan and receive potential suggestions. I am not wild about the idea but feel that I have little to lose. During our meeting, the individual from Organizational Development described his role as a development coach. The coach challenged my development plan. At the end of the session, the coach shared an audio book on effective leadership transition. I am flying out next Monday morning for business, so I will have the time on the plane to listen to the CD.

> ## *"The coach challenged my development plan."*

Late April

The book on making an effective leadership transition really made me think. It provided many useful insights for the types of challenges I have been struggling with in my new role. I went out over the weekend and bought my own hard copy of the book and marked up a couple of chapters that were of particular interest. My development coach sent me an e-mail to inquire whether the CD was helpful and to continue our last discussion.

May

While meeting with my development coach, we discussed, among other ideas, an assimilation process that involves my entire team of direct reports. It seems interesting and promises to jump-start the discussion of changes to the business that I see coming. My development coach shared that this assimilation process was originated in the military and is used by many leading companies with individuals who take on new and significant responsibilities leading others. I decided to embrace this approach.

> *"It seems interesting and promises to jump-start the discussion of changes to the business I see coming."*

Mid-May

The assimilation process was very helpful and the four hours we invested was really well spent. A number of issues were discussed that will make for better team dynamics and several items surfaced from team members. It was a good opportunity to get everyone aligned and working more effectively as a unit.

Late June

My development coach wants to touch base and discuss my progress. He had previously mentioned a program offered by a local university; thus far I have not enrolled. We explored me enrolling now for the September session to secure a spot. Fall is good timing for me, so I enrolled on their web site and received my confirmation the next day.

September

I just attended the one-day workshop at a nearby university. It felt sort of funny being on a college campus again. I got lots of useful information from the session. The class was filled with peers from companies dealing with the same issues in their business. One person in particular was from a pharmaceutical company and we seemed to hit it off during the break-out sessions. He agreed to meet over lunch in the near future and provide suggestions since his company is further along in their learning curve. The experience made me realize it is good to step away from an issue for a short time and to obtain new and different perspectives that can remedy the problem.

Late September

As another quarter comes to a close, it comes as no surprise that I have a voicemail from my development coach. He suggested meeting again to review progress with my development plan. I have to admit how things change. I was pretty skeptical at first about development plans and went along only because I couldn't really come up with an excuse to get out of completing development objectives. I also thought the development discussions would be an annoyance and that I would have precious little time to devote to my development. As the year winds down, I've made good headway in my areas for development and more importantly, I sense that I am becoming more effective at leadership. During our meeting I had to admit that trying to stretch my capabilities reinforced my resolve to become better and to learn more. My coach then asked me about my opportunity to participate in a 360 degree leadership survey. The primary benefit of the 360 review will be feedback from a wide range of perspectives and will facilitate sharing information about my leadership style and skill sets that aren't necessarily positive. I hesitate to commit; I agreed to think about it.

Late October

I decided to move forward with the 360 feedback session. After some thought, I am curious to determine whether there are gaps in how my new team, new peers, and new boss perceive me versus how I view myself.

As I reviewed the results of the 360 assessment, I see some real gaps and differences of opinion on my leadership capabilities and style. I also now realize that I want to work on certain specific areas such as my presentation skills, which I will call out in my development objectives for next year.

December

My development coach and I are meeting for the last time this year. We discussed that as the year progressed, I had purposely invested time and effort in completing my development objectives. This investment of time and energy has enabled me to deliver stronger results and to complete one of the most successful years of my career. I believe I am well-positioned for the upcoming year, as well as ready to take on new roles in the future. Because of the push from my development coach along the way, I now am much better equipped to handle the ever-changing business challenges.

> *"Because of the push from my development coach along the way, I now am much better equipped to handle the ever-changing business challenges."*

DESIGNING ACCELERATED PROFESSIONAL DEVELOPMENT PLANS

Clearly, some of the most important work of a development coach is in assisting leaders with accelerated development as they transition to new situations or roles. Development requires change, especially as an individual advances through the organization and as the scope and complexity of their role increases. Some leaders may be incapable of making the transition if they rely on their past experiences; ironically they become victimized by their own success. In these cases, by looking into past success and performance they ignore new demands and their performance falters. Consequently, a successful leader reflects on and explores the following areas for transition with their coach:

- What knowledge and which specific competencies are most important to success?
- What development activities are aligned with these competencies?
- What do I want to know and what will increase my chances for success now?

Perhaps most rewarding is when a person placed in a highly visible assignment provides feedback regarding their investment in coaching and its role in their success. One example follows:

"Recently, I have had the privilege of working with the Organizational Development Team both before and after my transition into my new leadership role. On the front end, we spent time discussing ideas from the publication "*The First 90 Days*" by Michael Watkins and the impact these concepts could have on my success. The exploration gave me good insight into some of the challenges that I might, and ultimately did, face. It empowered me to structure an effective strategy for asserting my leadership and taking control of a new role with the full support of my direct reports. It also helped prioritize and focus my attention on the key needs during those first critical weeks.

I knew I was on the right track when after only a few days in my new office, the first mail arrived and I found another copy of the book, *The First 90 Days*, from a mentor who is a General Manager of a life science sister company like Sigma-Aldrich. My friend commented that he found the book useful during his transition to manage a foreign subsidiary and strongly suggested it to me to shorten my learning curve and avoid some of the common mistakes that many new managers make.

Of course, I knew that getting past the first 90 days in my new role was just the beginning. I was happy to have the continued assistance of my development coach to help me monitor my progress and make certain I remained on the right track for the long term. Working in a different culture and with a staff that had recently gone through an unexpected organizational change, it was difficult to know if I was getting accurate feedback or not. Having a secure and impartial environment in which to collect and explore constructive feedback has been very important.

> *"I was happy to have the continued assistance of my development coach..."*

My team's conference with a neutral facilitator allowed me to receive critical feedback and enabled a discussion forum for remaining issues, clearing them and allowing us to move forward in sync as a new leadership team. I found the tools offered by our Organizational Development Team to be very useful. These processes have been tested and successfully deployed by many leading companies and it makes sense to employ them at Sigma-Aldrich to reduce the learning curve." - *Managing Director, Sigma-Aldrich Corporation*

187

WHAT ORGANIZATIONAL LEADERS CAN LEARN FROM COACHING RELATIONSHIPS

Most of us can look back and readily identify coaches who have had a significant and positive impact on our careers. These coaches were able to see us at our very best and to challenge us to examine our skills, talents, and aspirations. These coaches were able to focus our attention on such critical issues and questions as:

- Are you doing your very best work right now?
- What do you want to improve?
- What will achieving this improvement do for you and the business?
- What is stopping your from improving your performance?
- How are you getting in your own way?
- How are you going to get there?

Just as research and development are essential for continued scientific excellence, likewise coaching is vital to leverage the organization's human capital. The development and coaching of employees are also increasingly important to attract and retain outstanding talent. So in the process of being coached, organizational leaders better learn and model management skills in their day-to-day interactions with others. Further, their own coaching process results in a discovery process as to what constitutes effective coaching and development of their subordinates.

> *"...coaching is vital to leverage the organization's human capital."*

For example, this discovery process may result in reflections that incorporate the following:

- Coaching isn't something you do to employees - it's something you do <u>with</u> employees
- Subordinates are capable and creative
- Coaching isn't an occasional conversation - it's a continuous process
- Subordinates will be more motivated when working from a mutually agreed upon agenda
- The working relationship between a manager and his/her subordinates requires mutual respect, rapport, and honesty

There is a wide range of performance levels among subordinates within a work group. In Sigma-Aldrich's performance management system, a five point scale is used as follows:

5 - Consistently and significantly exceeds performance expectations

4 - Consistently meets all and exceeds some performance expectations

3 - Consistently meets all performance expectations

2 - Consistently meets most, but not all performance expectations

1 - Consistently fails to meet performance expectations

Every subordinate's performance is somewhere on the continuum of ratings and the leader's job is all about moving performance further along the continuum in the direction of high performance. Standing still equates to falling behind the competition.

Perhaps most important, the potential benefit when organizational leaders receive coaching is development and reinforcement of several essential management skills such as:

1. Building mutual respect and trust
2. Providing regular supportive and constructive feedback
3. Asking effective questions
4. Creating and implementing a development plan for each subordinate

1. Building mutual respect and trust

It is essential to build mutual respect and trust so employees want to work with their leaders. With trust, employees are more willing to hear and act on the big picture and strategy of their leaders. Other advantages are that subordinates will be more willing to talk openly and there will be a higher degree of candor in the relationship. Trust starts at the beginning of any relationship and builds over time so it is a process rather than an event.

Further, in today's knowledge-based environment, one cannot coach someone without their permission. Coaching and performance improvement are built on a trusting relationship in which the leader as a coach is welcomed into a relationship to create and sustain business results. Leaders only earn this welcome when they create the right environment built on trust and mutual respect.

> *"Coaching and performance improvement are built on a trusting relationship..."*

2. Providing regular supportive and constructive feedback

Feedback is ideally given on a regular basis to all subordinates regardless of their level of performance. This sort of consistency prevents frustration on the part of both the employees and manager when employees don't know what to expect from their manager and the manager doesn't understand why the employee isn't improving. Further, the leader must strike a balance between reinforcing feedback and redirecting feedback.

Reinforcing Feedback	Redirecting Feedback
-Recognition for a job well done	-Redirecting behavior
-Recognize improvement in performance or progress towards mastery	-Makes employee aware of a skill enhancement opportunity or a potential problem area
-Recognize extra effort	-Encourages behavior to change
-Recognize assistance given others	-Points out when an expectation or business standard is not being met
-Encourage the same behavior in the future	-Helps an employee be more effective (behavior is directionally correct but there is a better way of doing it)
-Encourage so that good performance will continue	

Coaching leaders means that when providing redirecting feedback they are aware and use judgment to deliver it when it is of maximum benefit for the person receiving the feedback. By providing it in this timeframe, the feedback is more likely to be viewed as helpful rather than criticism.

Closely related to feedback is the concept of dialogue. Feedback can be one-way communication where the leader is giving information to the employee about his/her performance. Dialogue, on the other hand, invites the employee to discuss his/her own performance. The employee plays the active role and identifies:

- What he/she is doing well
- What needs improvement
- Ideas for how to improve performance

The benefits of the employee identifying areas and ways for improvement follow:

- Employee is an owner in his/her own development

- Employee has ownership for successes and opportunities
- Employee has ownership for future actions, including solutions for improving performance

3. Asking effective questions

A job-description of a leader is incomplete without the inclusion of asking effective questions. This is a skill that must be honed and perfected and this is most effectively done with coaching. Leaders who produce the best results in business are those likely to say "let's inquire into that" rather than impose their opinion. By asking questions, it sends a signal that getting results is a collaborative process and that mutual learning is valued.

Asking questions elicits important information and provides other benefits as well such as encouraging active listening, helping build trust, encouraging involvement and ownership, and offering support without removing responsibility.

> *"A job-description of a leader is incomplete without inclusion of asking effective questions."*

4. Creating and implementing a development plan for each subordinate

Employees are unique and leaders that vary their approach for each subordinate are more effective. This requires that he/she think through opportunities to improve each individual which occurs most effectively with coaching. Sigma-Aldrich emphasizes that all development plans reflect a 70-20-10 blend meaning:

- 70 percent of development is based on experience within the current assignment
- 20 percent of development is based on learning from others
- 10 percent of development is from classroom training, web-based training, self-study, etc.

While every employee's opportunities for improvement are different, the common themes for development planning are as follows:

- Strategic (positive impact on current deliverables and/or future roles)
- Targeted (focused on one or two areas)
- Follows the 70-20-10 blend concept (the majority of the plan must be grounded in and connect development activities to real work and then fill in the remainder of the plan with selected workshops or mentoring/learning from others)
- Project-based and execution focused (specific due dates and milestones)
- Shared responsibility and accountability (employee owns the process and others will assist and support – particularly the direct manager who asks for regular updates)

In summary, the coaching received by organizational leaders spurs and reinforces transferable skills that contribute to more effective leadership. This, in turn, assists in the development of their respective subordinates, their team, and themselves.

LESSONS LEARNED

There are a number of lessons to be learned in the process of development planning.

First, leaders who take the time to create their own formal development plan and have coaching are far more likely to succeed in their improvement efforts. Writing a plan is the first step in getting started. Finding time to formalize the development plan and then working the plan are both key to staying motivated.

Second, take the wide variety of learning styles into account. Some leaders prefer to learn by doing and experiencing things first-hand. Others prefer formal classes followed by discussion and debriefing. Some prefer self-study and reading. In reality, all are valuable and are ideally implemented in a blended fashion with coaching. The precise mix and sequence may be different for each individual leader. Assignment-based development is essential to prevent an event mentality in which development relies on classroom training then lacks follow through. Examples of job or assignment-based development grounded in the leader's day-to-day experience include stretch assignments such as an increase in scope or complexity of the present assignment, special or fix-it projects, and/or project team leadership. Experience-based development can be supplemented by learning from others, coaching, formal training programs, 360 degree surveys, etc.

Thirdly, to create accountability, it is best to involve the direct manager of the leader in the development plan process. The direct manager contributes practical ideas regarding effective and efficient ways to learn and apply new capabilities, and identifies the area(s) of development that will add the greatest value. They also supply the financial investment that may be required in support of their employee's development plan. Further, the direct manager is familiar with the knowledge and skill set that will be required as their subordinates move to their next level responsibility. They provide insight on changes in expectation, skill sets, and the complexities their subordinates will be required to successfully navigate their next job assignment.

Finally, the Sigma-Aldrich leadership approach places a high priority on feedback and knowing oneself. The environment encourages and facilitates external assessments that provide detailed information on leadership style and makes 360 degree assessments available to leaders on a voluntary basis. It is difficult, at best, to lead and understand others when one doesn't really understand their own leadership strengths and weaknesses. Because the 360 degree feedback survey provides information about how the leader's peers, superiors, and employees view their skills and leadership style, this information is critical to gaining greater insight, self-discovery, and growth. It is also very helpful in narrowing the strengths and areas for improvement that a leader commits to further develop. Research shows that a 360 without coaching is more often detrimental while having a coach provides positive results following the feedback.

> *"Research shows that a 360 without coaching is more often detrimental while having a coach provides positive results following the feedback."*

Overall, the lessons learned in development planning at Sigma-Aldrich are:

- Development plans must be documented and treated as any other business commitment

195

- Development plans must be customized for each individual leader
- Development plans must be balanced among types of learning activities and between strengths and areas for improvement
- Development plans must be highly-focused and realistic regarding the degree and pace of change - leaders cannot change too many things at once or completely remake themselves in a matter of months
- The direct manager of the leader must be involved to create shared ownership and accountability, ensure development objectives are aligned with business requirements, and encourage the leader to continuously grow and expand contributions in the future
- Self-knowledge is invaluable and creates the awareness of the gap between the current and desired state, driving motivation for change and improvement

SIGMA-ALDRICH LEADERSHIP DEVELOPMENT SUMMARY

Successful outcomes from coaching are a partnership among the leader, his/her manger, and the development coach.

It is the leader's responsibility to:

- Develop and document development plans
- Implement plans by monitoring progress and staying on course
- Develop a clear understanding of talents, interests, and goals

The leader's manager has responsibility to:

- Work with subordinates to find opportunities to grow and expand their contributions

196

- Provide or help subordinates to locate the tools, resources, information, and feedback required to implement their development plans
- Be available for development conversations and provide support/recognition for progress

Each development coach has the responsibility to:

- Be a catalyst for self-reflection
- Provide another perspective
- Be objective and candid
- Explore opportunities and development ideas as appropriate

The desired outcome maximizes the benefits to both the individual leader and Sigma-Aldrich Corporation. Each development plan is a targeted investment in the human capital of the organization. To create sustainable value, Sigma-Aldrich continues proactively developing its talent and providing coaching, ensuring that the required capabilities are in place to successfully execute strategy and capitalize on growth opportunities.

Erick Koshner is an Organizational Development Manager for Sigma-Aldrich Corporation and resides in St. Louis, Missouri. Erick has over thirty years of experience in human resources and organizational development with major companies ranging from Monsanto, Eastman Chemical, Citigroup, as well as Sigma-Aldrich Corporation. Erick's expertise is in the areas of leadership development, succession planning, change management, employee engagement, and coaching.

Erick is a Certified Professional Coach through the Center of Coaching Certification. At Sigma-Aldrich, a leading Life Science and High Technology Company with approximately 10,000 employees in 40 countries, he works with a select talent pool and utilizes coaching skills to support as well as challenge others to achieve their full potential. He can share broad organizational perspective and learning from working with hundreds of successful leaders/executives.

Erick holds an M.A. in Industrial Psychology from the University of Minnesota and is certified in a variety of diagnostic and training tools including the Lominger Suite, Creative Metrics, Myers-Briggs Type Indicator, Wilson Learning, Forum, Interaction Associates, Targeted Learning, Communispond, Career Systems, Achieve Global, and Development Dimensions International.

He and his wife, Theresa, enjoy gardening and travelling to visit their adult children.

erick.koshner@sial.com
ekoshner@aol.com

MOVING BEYOND METRICS WITH PERFORMANCE BASED COACHING

Jeanne Hathcock

The combination of today's economic climate and the developing savvy consumer requires the need for disciplined execution in all areas of corporate performance and in all genres of business.

Customers are smarter, better versed, and more demanding than ever. The sense of entitlement continues to be prevalent in our culture and when combined with the increased options available to every consumer, demands and expectations continue to escalate at an alarming rate. At first glance, meeting customer demand and requirements may seem unattainable in our current culture. The truth is, it's doable! There are many tools available today that support performance development in all areas of business, from customer service to product delivery. Striving to find the right tools for our business and customer needs is key to being successful today and being a contender 10 years from now for the market share enjoyed currently. Using strategic development of product and individuals, combined with disciplined execution, will enhance the odds at retaining the market share currently achieved while effectively positioning the business to take on future market share with the help and support of satisfied and developed employees.

How can we meet the growing demands of our customers while strengthening and growing our market share? We can work hard, put in "a good days work", and try, try, try... let's be honest here. At the end of the day the effort and/or energy simply doesn't get the job done in a way that maximizes customer service while delivering the results the company needs to stay in business. Today's customer expects and demands more. They want options and they want to know all of them right now! They want to talk to a "live" person without listening to the auto attendant options available to get to the person most equipped to meet their needs. The upcoming generation may not be as interested in talking to a live person; they want minimal effort into reading the tutorials or FAQ's on how to find the information or product. The wants of the consumer go on and on.

Performance based coaching supports the employee through embarking on a collaborative journey of learning, developing, and monitoring all aspects of performance. Improved communication, partnered with increased product knowledge and proven sales and service techniques moves performance behaviors in a positive direction. It doesn't matter whether the employee is at the bottom, middle, or top of the metric chart. Long term performance coaching eliminates identified roadblocks and the ceiling of effort, moving past the barriers between will and skill, opening an unlimited pathway of potential for the employee and the organization they support.

> *"Performance based coaching supports the employee through embarking on a collaborative journey of learning, developing, and monitoring all aspects of performance."*

In the three years I have been solely focused on improving performance, both behavioral and technical, I have watched employees improve job satisfaction, develop new skills, and significantly improve corporate ability to meet customer demand while increasing satisfaction. I have personally witnessed numerous success stories of employees achieving personal and professional results they hadn't thought were possible. I have seen an increase in sales, improved customer service, and employee empowerment. During this same time, I reviewed numerous employee surveys confirming an increase in overall employee satisfaction. In a few short years, I have watched our sales organization shift from an "order taker" mindset to a sales approach that lets customers know we want and value their business and loyalty. We are still on the journey, committed to refining our skills and increasing our developmental opportunities as we move toward a goal of being a world class organization, providing superior product, service, and customer satisfaction.

How Coaching Impacts Performance

Performance coaching directly impacts an organization's bottom line in a multitude of ways. If you are reading this book, you already know or have heard the various industry statistics that promote the positive contributions of performance coaching and coaching in general. I won't bore you with more industry statistics; I will tell you that I have personally witnessed our sales and service teams take on aspirational performance targets that were 2 times the current productivity levels and blow those targets away in less than a year in most cases, and then continue to sustain or grow beyond those targets to achieve even greater success and satisfaction. These improvements are not simply the result of working harder. It is the reward of investing in sustainable improvements by working smarter and by working together. Through collaborative learning, coaching, and standardization, employees achieved greater performance results, enjoyed increased job satisfaction, and took ownership and pride in the service they provided their customers and organization. This is still their mindset three years later and they recognize through their performance coaching the only ceiling they have is the one they put on themselves and their own abilities. They recognize and welcome working for an organization that supports and invests in them. In this chapter I am going to focus on just a few of the ways performance coaching has positively impacted employees and organizations.

The first proven tool of performance coaching is knowledge. You have heard it said that knowledge is power and vice versa. Collaborative performance coaching unleashes the knowledge base and capability of both the coach and the coachee. For example, if I am coaching someone to improve their product knowledge and to support them in increasing their sales performance, I must know about or have access to the full range of products and services available to this coachee. This knowledge, combined with my coaching abilities, will assist the coachee in maximizing their selling potential.

> *"Collaborative performance coaching unleashes the knowledge base and capability of both the coach and the coachee."*

Next, full understanding and disclosure of the identified performance metric is critical to the long-term success of the coaching relationship. The first step in identifying the performance gap is to understand both the current level and the desired performance to meet customer demand. The ideal place to start a dialog on performance expectations is for the coach and the coachee to review the strategic goals of the company and how those goals support the organization's mission, vision, and values.

Understanding what the company is about and where it is going supports understanding the performance expectations for everyone within the organization. Then explore potential performance gaps between the job expectation and the current delivered results. With a mutually agreed upon understanding of the expectations, the coachee and coach will move forward together identifying the roadblocks, opportunities for moving past the barriers to bridge the performance gap, and support the employee in achieving the next level. Strategic corporate goals are often stretch goals and require employees to work through process improvement initiatives as well as identify best practices in their daily work to reach the goals. Combining process improvement with performance coaching pushes the ceiling upward on what is truly achievable for individual employees as well as the organization. Engaging the coach and the coachee to strive for continuous improvement births new possibilities and opportunities for the organization to grow and expand beyond the goals and objectives set. Additionally, the knowledge gained from collaborative learning through coaching provides a springboard effect to identifying best practices as well as pitfalls, allowing other employees to gain insights from coaching partnerships.

One vision. One goal. To maximize performance coaching, there must be an established vision or goal that is bigger than the coach and the coachee. This vision and goal must be understood and embraced in the performance coaching relationship, with both participants having ownership and responsibility in the bigger vision and goals of the organization. Embracing the corporate vision and goals allows the coach and coachee to immediately focus on what skills, tools, knowledge, and development is required to achieve the established targets and goals. The coach and coachee will have a clearer understanding of what is expected of them, and how their coaching relationship supports the organization and amplifies the vision statement because of their own personal performance. Performance coaching effectively communicates the desired results, the intention of the coaching partnership, and develops a collaborative learning style between the coach and the coachee to ensure maximum success and results. One way of gauging the success of performance coaching is to track the daily, weekly, or monthly performance of the coachee. Using a coaching development plan to document the performance goals previously achieved and the new targets agreed upon creates a transparent culture of real time performance management. The coach and the coachee are then aware of the performance successes and the potential gaps that may be present. Ideally, a performance development plan also contains the current action steps being implemented by the coachee to support reaching the identified performance targets. Often the coach is also a mentor with the responsibility of monitoring the identified behaviors to provide feedback, both positive and constructive, on how the coachee is progressing toward their goal. The coach and the coachee equally share in the successes and take individual responsibility for their actions within the relationship.

Effective Performance Coaching Partnerships

A healthy coaching partnership is critical to the long-term success of performance coaching. Unlike the more traditional coaching relationship, where a coach may meet with a client for an hour once a week, the performance coach is center stage at all times. Their team members represent the group requirements to which the performance coach is accountable for. This is where collaborative coaching becomes crucial.

The performance coach must know how to balance their own and their team's performance accountability. This requires the performance coach to role model the desired behaviors and necessary actions required of their team members to achieve the agreed upon targets and objectives. In other words, the coachee achieves success with the coach and vice versa. This is why the coaching partnership is so critical to the long-term success of the employee and the organization.

An effective performance coaching partnership requires trust and rapport. Long term success and development requires the coach and coachee to agree on attainable stretch targets and goals. These targets must be supported with positive and frequent communication as well as a strong, personal vision that further supports the overall strategic goals and the corporate vision or mission statement. Providing team members with an understanding of the correlation between the company based goals and objectives and how their team and personal goals and objectives supports the bigger picture is the cornerstone to performance coaching. For example: If I am a customer service representative within my organization and one of the strategic goals identified is to improve customer service survey results, I need to know and understand the survey questions the customers are asked to respond to in order to successfully achieve the higher scores my organization is striving to obtain. My performance coach will work with me to ensure I have a full understanding of the survey questions asked of my customers, and we will work together to explore new tools and ways to enhance my performance in a way that positively impacts my overall survey scores. By utilizing a performance coaching development plan, my coach and I will monitor the progress made on improving my survey scores, identifying best practices or performance gaps.

"An effective performance coaching partnership requires trust and rapport."

Preferred communication styles like VAK (Visual / Auditory / Kinesthetic) are welcome tools of the performance coach. Understanding the communication style of the coachee (do they see, hear, or feel their way through learning) supports powerful dialog and helps build trust and understanding within the coaching relationship. Coaches that adapt their communication style to the learning style of their coachee build trust faster and have more satisfying and motivating dialog. Effective performance coaches understand the more powerful the communication is between them and their team, the better the performance.

In a recent coaching skills class, a coaching pre-work assignment required the coach to reflect on the communication style of their coachee. Several of the coaches indicated they were surprised at how much they had to concentrate and listen to identify their coachee's preferred learning style. As we reviewed VAK, the class participants identified several examples of how much more effective they could have been and will be as they begin practicing how to identify preferred communication styles.

This is one example of how enhanced listening skills are foundational and necessary to identify and improve individual and team performance. Listening to understand, listening for roadblocks, and development interests that support performance improvement is a constant part of the coaching process.

Self-assessment also plays a key role in the performance coaching partnership. The coachee must learn how to evaluate and articulate their own performance in order to identify areas of opportunity for further development. It is the coach's role to ensure regular self-reflection occurs and the coachee independently identifies the opportunities for improvement.

Just as the coachee has performance requirements that must be met, so does the coach as a team leader. A healthy performance coaching partnership allows open communication and dialog to occur about the goals and objectives of the coachee, the team and, ultimately, the coach. A regular cadence of communication that expresses the current status of the targets, rolling up to the corporate initiatives, keeps the focus on the process and not on the individual.

If the individual becomes the roadblock to success, then behavioral coaching would be substituted for performance coaching. Behavioral coaching, of course, is a whole different topic in-and-of-its-self. Situations occur in any genre of coaching where the coachee's personal behavior becomes the road block to success. Some examples of behavioral roadblocks could be attitude, confidence, desire, accountability, etc. The performance coach is ever mindful of understanding the root causes associated with any performance gaps their coachee may be experiencing. It is important in the performance coaching relationship for the coach to identify and communicate with the coachee when it is appropriate to shift the focus to behavioral coaching and the reasons. This gives the coachee an opportunity to openly discuss with their coach the root causes of the behavioral road block. This discussion ideally leads to a clear and agreed upon action plan on how the coachee will work toward overcoming their behavioral roadblock, positioning them to once again focus on their performance.

CONDUCTING AN EFFECTIVE COACHING SESSION
– THE COLLABORATIVE COACH / INTERPERSONAL SKILLS

Preparing for coaching sessions is a foundational requirement for a successful coaching engagement. Understanding the coachee's previous and present performance behavior gives the coach credibility in the coaching session. It is important for the coachee to know their coach understands where they have been and where they are currently headed.

Frequently the path of least resistance can be to engage in anything but coaching! There is always a time and place for instructing, mentoring, and counseling an employee. The performance coaching session is not one of those places or time. The performance coach must resist every temptation to tell the employee what they are doing wrong or what they need to do to improve. This is where the term, Collaborative Coach, comes into play.

> *"It is important for the coachee to know their coach understands where they have been and where they are currently headed."*

We discussed earlier the importance of self-assessment. Although a regular cadence of performance overviews between the coach and the coachee is crucial, the coach guides the coachee through a self-assessment of where they see their own performance gaps and the areas of performance that are going well. As the collaborative coach, it is imperative to ask open-ended questions that support the coachee's self-assessment as well as offer perspective on what action plans can be implemented to address the performance gaps.

How the coach communicates their observations and possible ideas will determine the effectiveness of the coaching session. The coach must be prepared to share best practices, explore potential options, and offer their support in overcoming obstacles.

The use of VAK, silence, and listening techniques become critical in the one-to-one coaching relationship. The better the communication is the more effective the performance development. It takes discipline and practice. Stick with it! Knowing and understanding what tools are available as a coach will support moving past the roadblocks standing between the current state and the desired performance. If the coachee requires refresher training on specific products or processes, what are the resources? A successful coach knows where to find and how to use available resources. For example, if a coachee wants access to certain types of information to enhance their response effectiveness, what support could a system administrator offer to assess whether the access will indeed assist the coachee in their performance development?

The final critical component of the effective coaching session is the summarization of the discussion and the agreed upon action plan. A performance-based coaching session is successful when an action plan is identified, communicated, and agreed upon. This action plan ideally outlines specific objectives as well as a way to measure the success of the objective. The action plan is developed by the coachee with the coach serving as a partner in the process.

Example: There was a young man who worked in phone sales who had an accent. The employee identified their accent as a potential roadblock to improving their sales. His coach supported this observation and worked with him to improve his communication style on the phone. Specifically, they worked on identifying words that were difficult to understand and replaced them with words that were easier to understand with his accent. They worked together to identify how to gather as much information as possible from the customer using the fewest words while keeping the customer engaged. This collaborative effort paid off! The young man improved his sales ratio and both he and the coach were able to personally witness the effectiveness of collaborative coaching and the positive impact it can have on both the coachee and the organization.

> *"A performance-based coaching session is successful when an action plan is identified, communicated, and agreed upon."*

COACHING THE COACH

Performance based coaching can be demanding. It requires concentrated attention to details, individual coaching opportunities, and understanding the big picture of the team. To be an effective performance-based coach, it is critical to have regular coach observations for continued development and direction.

Most performance-based organizations provide bonuses or incentives when specific metrics and targets are met. The coach is constantly communicating how improved performance personally benefits the coachee. The coach also is reminded of the reasons they are providing the performance coaching.

The coach's coach is available on a regular basis to observe the performance coach preparing, interacting, and following up with their coachee. The role of this special coach is to provide support, perspective, and coaching development for the performance coach. In addition, this specialized coach is following up with the performance coach to ensure they are following through on the identified action plans for themselves as well as their team members. One of the roles of the observer coach is to listen for key words that help identify the communication style of the performance coach. Another critical role of the coaching observer is to role model the coaching behaviors necessary to successfully improve performance. This allows the performance coach to see specific behaviors role modeled for them as well as capturing additional best practices and different viewpoints.

One of the most common challenges I see while observing coaching is the coaches struggling to be fully present and engaged with the coachee. Often times a phone is ringing, an instant message demands an immediate response, or another team member unknowingly walks in on a coaching session, interrupting the dynamic of the session or the thoughts of the coach and/or coachee. When I am providing feedback to the coach after the session, I point out the importance of being fully present and I make sure my phone is sent directly to voicemail, my instant messaging is turned off, and either my door is closed or I have a visual sign displayed identifying that I am unavailable at this time unless it is an emergency, etc. This gives me, the observer coach, credibility to what I am coaching to as well as providing best practice examples to the coach by allowing them to see that everyone has interruptions they must contend with.

Many companies, like my own, require a coaching certification process for all their coaches. This certification process ensures the tools and concepts taught in coaching are applied on the job as well as assessing how well the tools and concepts are working within the operation. Sometimes, the observer coach will take on the responsibility of certifying coaches. Coaching certification is also a topic of its own for another time and chapter.

Performance coaching works! If your team is struggling to meet performance requirements or you simply want to see what your team is capable of doing, consider introducing performance coaching to your organization. Putting together an implementation strategy that focuses on the benefits of coaching and what the desired outcome of the coaching are to be will ensure a supportive and positive program roll out. There are plenty of coaching professionals available to assist with putting the right program together for your team to enhance the performance of your team. Start exploring what your team could be doing and what they are able to accomplish. Reach out to affordable professionals who can assist you. The Center for Coaching Certification provides training, tools, and resources that will meet your requirements and the Coaching Skills for Leaders program that includes everything for you to train coaches. The benefits of performance based coaching far outweigh the costs associated with acquiring the skills and training required for improving performance.

"Performance coaching works!"

It is my hope you have found this chapter insightful and encouraging. Getting on the journey is the biggest step you will take toward improving your own performance and that of your team. You deserve the best for your organization and for the employees you support. Like me, I hope you will decide to take the journey as well and discover your full potential. My best to you and your team!

"Getting on the journey is the biggest step you will take toward improving your own performance and that of your team."

 Jeanne Hathcock is a Global Lead Process Champion, responsible for leading global process improvements using a variety of industry tools, including monthly coaching and certification, Lean and Six Sigma. Focusing on process improvement and performance driven employee development has increased her organizations Sales Ratio objectives YOY and more than doubled the productivity in customer service response time. For the last five years, Jeanne has focused her extensive knowledge and skill set on coaching people to improve their performance in the areas of sales and service.

Coaching emphasis has been placed on process improvement, technical skills, and effective communication skills. In 2012, Jeanne will introduce a new global coaching program to her organization that will further drive improvements in the area of sales and service through the use of employee development plans, coaching certification requirements, and SMARTS objective action plans.

Prior to coaching, Jeanne has studied and mastered Lean and Six Sigma tools to support metric driven process improvement initiatives, including 8D problem solving, SIPOCS, Affinity Diagrams, Value Stream Mapping, and extensive charting and graphing of data. As a certified professional coach, Jeanne has the training and ability to help others meet their performance objectives.

jeannehathx@cox.net

a

Because of the success of the process for creating this book
and the quality of the content, each year the
Center for Coaching Certification invites
Certified Professional Coaches
to participate in writing a chapter
for another edition of Coaching Perspectives.
Watch for a new book each year
and consider participating as one of our trained coaches!

78006795R00125

Made in the USA
Columbia, SC
07 October 2017